Six Lives Left
Hey! Where Are My Shoes?

Thomas Neamtu

SIX LIVES LEFT

Hey! Where are my Shoes?

Thomas Neamtu

Thomas Neamtu

Copyright © 2024 by Thomas Neamtu

All rights reserved. If you happen to be inspired by the stories within and want to create your own content, please reach out for your intent on a collaboration.

First Printing, 2025

ISBN

Six Lives Left

This book is dedicated to

everyone who had to put up with the little monster I was.

Thank you,

for a well-deserved kick in the pants!

Contents

Introduction 9
Garden Hose Nightmare 10
What Flavor Is Blue 22
Apple Sauce 26
Lost Shoe Trouble 29
The Trouble with Third Grade 34
Scavenger Hunt 42
Rubber Band Launch 46
Now That's a Treasure 49
The Story of Boots 54
The Neighbor of Mr. Rogers 61
Teaching Ducks to Fly 66
The Adventures of Donald & Daffy 69
Second Chance for Trouble 73
Eye School 81
Shadow People 85
Camping is Fun 88
A Career in Forgery 93
Noodle Soup 98
Fair Exchange 105
Wet Socks 109
Island Fortress.. 112

Island Fortress Part Deux..117
No Cracks 122
Something That Can't Be Fixed...126
Bus Stop Adventures..129
Stupid Questions..135
The Wrong Door 140
Corner Store Contest..144
Pumpkin of Nightmares 148
A Visit from the Grinch..154
Pig Wrangler 162
The Iron Curtain 168
Static White Noise 178
Bike Trip 1995 – The Beginning 186
Bike Trip 1995 – Day One 189
Bike Trip 1995 – Day Two 195
Bike Trip 1995 – Day Three..202
Door Damage..205
Hiding in Plain Sight..213
Making Art 219
Demolition Derby...222
Just Like Dracula..227
If Looks Could Kill 236
Don't You Know Who I Am?..241

Check the Cord 247

Future Home of Strippers 251

The Next Adventure Was Super 254

You're Fired! 257

Only Once 259

Under New Management 265

Road to Exile 271

Unexpected Taxi Driver 278

Unexpected Lawyer Visit 282

Seeing Double 289

Master of Disaster 292

My First Roommate 297

Back in the Hole 301

Perfect Aim 305

A Family Connection 309

The End is Nigh 313

How Can Silence Be So Loud? 319

Facing the Ghosts 323

Two Weeks of Silence 328

Epilogue 335

Introduction

I have always loved movies. I attended my first movie when I was just a parasite inside my mother's belly. She waited in a darkened theatre to watch the 1979 "Alien." My still forming appendages flailing about inside her as she viewed the now classic film. She watched through her hand covered eyes, as the passengers lost in space were hunted by the newly formed and vicious creature. Her fingernails chewed to bloody stumps as the suspense built on screen. Her blood pumping faster into my new body from a well-timed on screen jump scare. I was hooked instantly. In mid November I hatched, ready to take on the world. Ready to be the legendary troublemaker that our family would laugh about for the decades to come.

These are just some of the stories of how I raised a little hell growing up and why I only have six lives left. Enjoy!

Hey! Where are my shoes?

Garden Hose Nightmare

I was the tiny villain of our street. No one was safe if I had the garden hose in my hands. The steady stream of water, blasting out the end of the green tube, was my weapon of choice. Once my small hands were strong enough to turn on the valve my reign of terror began.

I was handed the hose one day and instructed to water the flowers in moms' garden. I watered everything but the flowers. The water was launched into the sky, returning to the ground with a loud splatter. The water from the hose pouring out in a limp arc. Dad showed me how to position my thumb over the exiting water to build up some pressure. Then I finally got some force behind the flow. I immediately turned the hose on him, soaking his work clothes. The water was quickly shut off and the flowless hose was taken away. But in that moment, I understood the mischievous power of the garden hose.

I was always on the hunt for the valves that held back the invisible flow of the garden hose. I found one of the valves across the alley at the neighbor's house and made use of it regularly.

When I was six years old, I would wander out of our yard. I would shuffle across the gravel alley, kicking up dust, watching the rocks bounce along the ground. I liked to visit the old guy that lived on the other side of the road. His garage door was always open, and Dalton would be working on his seemingly endless supply of daily projects. I was welcomed into the garage with an opportunity to watch what he was doing, and some days even given the chance to help. I was always allowed to rummage in the toolbox, searching to find my favorite tool, the orange rubber mallet. On more than one occasion while I was using the rubber hammer, to bash things on the ground, the rubber would bounce back and knock me in the head.

Dalton would look down at me, as I worked on the ground, and say, "You better not start crying" he warned "If you're going to be stupid, you better be tough."

I would hold back any possibility of the tears that started to form around my eyes. I was more surprised by the sudden thump in the head, than any kind of pain. I wasn't the sort of child that just bursts into tears anyway. I abandoned the mallet on the floor and went over to the workbench.

I pulled up a step stool to get some extra height to see what he had being worked on. Dalton had taken apart a boat pump and had its parts spread out all over the place. The boat was parked in the garage over the winter, waiting for the next fishing trip. The boat had a deep blue paint with silver sparkles burred deep between the painted layers. The light that poured through the open garage door made it look like the boat was in reflective water even when it sat unsubmerged in the garage.

Dalton looked over to me and gave some instructions "Pass me that gasket," he pointed to my end of the bench.

I had no idea what a gasket was, so I hovered my hand over the spread-out parts until he would bark "That one."

My small fingers pinched the rubber circle and handed it over. I stood next to him for the next half hour as the parts started to get reassembled and disappear off the tabletop.

Once the pump was reassembled, Dalton looked up at the clock and declared, "looks like its time for a soda pop." "You want one?" he asked.

"Yes please, I like the pink one." I asked with excitement.

"Perfect, I will be right back." Dalton said.

Dalton walked out of the garage and down the stone path to the back door of his house go get the sodas. He always had the fridge in the basement stocked with a multitude of flavors. The ice-cold sodas were in glass bottles and my favorite was the pink cream soda.

Before he made it to the door of the house, I was making my way down the stone trail. Next to the screen door was the garden hose. It was bright green and when unravelled could reach all the corners of the yard. There was a silver nozzle attached to the hose, and it had grabbed my attention. I pulled at the nozzle and two wraps of the hose fell off the steel holder. I squeezed the front of the nozzle back, my small hand just being able to pull it tight to the handle. The hose was off and empty, no water sprayed out the end, just then Dalton returned holding the soda pops.

"Don't play with that," he said. "Let's go have our drinks," he indicated back to the garage.

"Ok," I agreed, putting the nozzle back on the hose wrap, the two fallen loops resting on the ground.

I ran back down the path towards the open garage door. Rushing inside to get to the folding chairs that waited, leaned up against the wall. We would setup the chairs behind the boat and watch the world go by as we enjoyed our cold drinks.

We had just finished our refreshments when my mother arrived to check on us.

"Hope Thomas wasn't causing any trouble over here," Mom said. Uncertain of the answer as it could have gone either way.

"No trouble at all," Dalton said. "He was a great little helper; we rebuilt the pump for the boat today."

"That sounds fun," mom said, "it's time for dinner Thomas, head on home."

I got up without any protest.

"See you tomorrow," I said to Dalton excitedly.

"I'm sure you will," Dalton laughed, as I wandered into his yard most days. Mom chuckled and we went home for our supper.

The next day I was quick to return to the garage, not wanting to miss out on the days project. The door was open, but the room was quiet. I walked out of the sunshine into the shade of the garage, the temperature outside was hot, and the transition felt nice.

"Hello?" I said quietly "are you in here Dalton?" I asked to no one.

The garage was empty. So, I started down the stone path towards the house. The sunshine glinted off the silver hose nozzle and caught my full attention. I went straight over to the hose. It had been rewrapped from the day before. I pulled the nozzle off the green coil and my eyes locked onto the valve. It was well within my reach, just above shoulder level. My small hand turned the valve with ease. The steel handle fitting perfectly in my grip. The hose instantly expanded as the water flowed in. I took two more loops off the hose rack and stood in front of the back door. I reached out a pressed the doorbell. I could hear the chimes inside, then a few heavy footsteps. The wooden door opened, and Dalton appeared.

"I got nothing to fix today, you should go home." He said.

Before he had a chance to focus on what I was holding, I squeezed the handle back on the nozzle. The blast of water shooting through the closed screen door and hitting Dalton right in the chest. He let out a surprised bellow of shock from the cold water.

I dropped the hose and was running home before the screen door even had a chance to be opened. Dalton stood at the back door shouting threats of violence as his soaked shirt dripped onto the floor.

I made it home in record time and went inside. My heart beating fast and my lungs burning from the run.

"I thought you were going to see if Dalton had any projects to work on?" Mom enquired as I went into the kitchen.

"Oh, he's not working on anything today." I explained. Not saying anything about the one-sided water fight we just had.

"Ok, you can go see him again tomorrow." Mom said unconcerned.

"Sure thing." I said and went off into the living room to plan out my next hose attack.

I returned to Dalton's yard the next day. The garage door was open, and he was not working at the bench again. This was going to work out great; I could pull the same trick as I had the day before. I was giggling to myself as I walked down the stone path. I got to the hose and noticed that the nozzle was missing. No problem I knew how to position my thumb over the end of the hose to get a good spray. I found the end of the hose and pulled it off the roll. I reached towards the valve; it was also missing. The tap was bare, just a square peg where the valve handle should have been. The valve handle was held in place by small screw and that was gone too. I replaced the hose and rang the doorbell. I could hear Dalton stomping inside the house as he approached the back door.

"Ah, you again?" He said. Looking over at the unravelled hose. "I'm not falling for that shit again." He smiled, pulling the valve handle from the unbuttoned pocket of his shirt. "This is going to stay safe, right here." Dalton said as he tapped the pocket.

"What are we going to do today?" I asked, trying to hide the disappointment of having my plans defeated.

"Have I got a job for you!" Dalton said with excitement.

"What is it?" I asked him with the same level of excitement.

"Come with me." He said as he opened the screen door. We walked across the grass back towards the garden that was next to the garage. "How do you feel about worms?" he asked.

"I don't mind worms." I said, "what do I got to do?" I asked.

The ground was wet from a rainstorm that happened over night. The garden was damp but not muddy.

"I'm gonna put these sticks in the ground" Dalton started to explain. "Hook them up to this battery, and when the worms come up you can put them in this tin can." He handed me a large empty coffee tin.

"Sure, I can do that." I said taking the can.

I investigated the tin, giving it a shake I could see the lost crumbs of coffee at the bottom.

Dalton walked over and pushed the sticks into the ground. Then he connected a wire from the two sticks to the battery.

Within a few seconds the ground wiggled as worms danced out of the dirt.

"I need as many as you can collect, I use them for bait, and we are going on a fishing trip this weekend." Dalton explained.

I got down on my knees and started to pluck the dancing worms from the earth. The first worms' body I touched shot out a spark and stung my fingers. I fell back onto the grass as Dalton laughed.

"Oh, you should have waited until I unhooked that battery or your gonna get zapped." Dalton laughed even harder at his late warning.

I looked up from the grass, angry, but I said nothing. I had fallen for his trick. Once the power was off, I went back to collecting the worms from the ground. The worms were not dangerous, so I scooped them into the tin without any worry. When the power was off, the worms just wiggled on top of the wet dirt, not knowing that they would soon be used as fish bait. After putting a hundred worms in the tin, I decided it was time to go back home.

"Thanks for collecting all the electric worms." Dalton said still chuckling at the trick that he played on me. "Will I see you tomorrow?" he asked, expecting me to decline the offer.

"You sure will." I said with a mischievous glint in my eye.

I then went back home to plot my revenge.

I got home and went straight down into the basement. Dad had a workshop down there. Just like his father, he collected and kept every used or broken part, just in case it might be needed for future use. I pulled up the step stool to the workbench. I stretched to reach the dangling string that would turn on the light. In the dark I missed the string on the first try, having to wait for it to swing back into my hand. The click of the switch was loud as the bulb illuminated.

I had seen the mechanism for my vengeance once before and now just needed to find it again. I knew what I was looking for. I had seen it in one of the clear plastic drawers Dad keeps the old parts in and I was going to put it back into service. I opened a few of the small drawers not knowing exactly where it was. After a few unsuccessful choices I found what I needed.

Dad had replaced our water valves outside the year before and had kept one of the broken handles. I pulled the broken valve handle out and gave it a quick inspection. I checked on the back to make sure it had the square hole needed to turn on the water. The valve handle was missing a third of the wheel, but the edges where it was broken were not that sharp. I put the piece of cast steel in my pocket for safe keeping. I made sure I closed the small drawer, covering my tracks. I reached up and pulled the string on the light, a loud click extinguished the bulb, then I went back upstairs.

Mom was in the kitchen. "What were you doing in the workshop?" she asked. She must have heard the unmistakable click of the pull string switch.

"I was just looking for something." I answered quickly.

"Well, stay out of there," she warned. "There are lots of sharp tools, and I don't want you to get cut." She explained.

"Ok" I said disappointed. Not telling her that I had already found what I was looking for.

I carried that broken valve wheel with me everywhere for the next few weeks. It rested in my pocket waiting for the right moment to be used. I now had the power to use any hose, anywhere.

A few weeks went by, the air was starting to cool down. School was going to be starting soon, my afternoons with Dalton were coming to an end. I decided today was going to be the day for vengeance, revenge for my electric worm zap.

I went into Dalton's yard and pulled the hose from the roll. I stretched the green coil out over towards the back step. The silver nozzle was back on the hose, but the valve handle was still missing. I rested the hose on the steps and went back to the water valve. I pulled the broken handle from my pocket. The square hole on the back fitting perfectly over the peg. I used both hands to turn the valve. The broken edge pressing into the palm of my hand. The valve was shut off tightly and took some effort to turn back on. I could hear as the water broke free from inside the house as it started to fill the hose. I put the valve handle back in my pocket and rushed over to the steps of the back door. I pressed the doorbell and quickly picked up the hose. The familiar sound of footsteps echoed inside the house. Dalton appeared as he opened the wooden inside door. He looked out at me with a smile. I looked back at him with a grin.

"Ah, nice try." He said. "I got the valve handle safe right here," as he tapped the shirt pocket.

I didn't say anything and just grinned like an idiot. I pulled the handle back on the nozzle and the water blasted out of the hose. The look of shock on his face as the water shot into the house was priceless. Before I had even had a chance to let go of the hose the screen door was open, and Dalton was out for blood. He was soaked. I dropped the hose and started to run home as fast as my short legs could carry me. I could run fast while being scared, but he could run faster while being angry. He caught up to me before I even left the yard. He swung his big boot towards my behind. The impact lifted me from the ground and propelled me further ahead, giving us some distance. We both raced across the gravel and into my yard. He was shouting of the violence and bodily harm he was going to do when he finally caught me, but I was quick and eluded his capture.

I got into the yard and ran towards the left side of the house. Dad had built us a playhouse over there and I thought it would provide me some safety. I entered the small wooden structure. The doorway was just big enough for me to fit through. I made it to the back wall, turning to look out.

Dalton was already at the door, reaching in, trying to pull me out. The doorframe was not wide enough for him to enter, so he only had one arm and shoulder inside. His arms were not long enough to reach me, as he tried to claw me out of the small house. After a few terrifying moments he retreated back into the depths of the yard and out of my sight.

I rested against the back wall, catching my breath, planning my escape. The hose water hit me directly in the face. The cold blast took my breath away. Dalton had retrieved the hose and was now trying to drown me out of the playhouse. I was instantly soaked and had nowhere to run or hide. I was trying to dodge the water, but the confined space made it impossible. I had wandered into his radius of reach and was pulled out from the playhouse with force. The hose was then jammed into the waistband of my pants, the ice-cold water burning as it soaked me from the inside out.

Mom rushed out of the house to see what the commotion was about. She managed to get out a "what's?" then stopped. Taking stock of the situation. The sight of a soaking wet sixty-year-old man with a garden hose down the pants of a six-year-old kid.

"I don't even want to know." She said holding back a laugh.

Dalton dropped the hose and said, "He started it!"

I picked up the hose and started to get him back. Dalton walked over to the valve and shut it off. I dropped the hose as the last of the water flowed out.

Mom laughed "Oh you too." "That's probably enough with the hose, eh?" "Thomas go get dried off."

Dalton looking defeated started to go home. "Little shit, started it."

Mom laughed and gave him assurance that she didn't doubt that I was the instigator, because I usually was.

I went in the house to find some dry clothes. Keeping the valve handle with me for safe keeping. I took that handle with me everywhere for months, but that was the last time I used it for some trickery, well at Dalton's house anyway.

What Flavor Is Blue

A few weeks after the hose incident, our family was invited over to Dalton's house for a birthday celebration. Dalton had survived another year and wanted to celebrate with some party cake and ice-cream. The gathering was taking place in the afternoon, so we got ready after lunch to attend the party. Before we left the house I was warned to be on my best behavior, I nodded with understanding. Mom looked at me with the "I know your up to something gaze." But didn't say anything.

We walked across the lane and into the house that was already full of people. I was given a hero's welcome. The news of my tricks on Dalton had generated me legendary status. I was moved around the room with a series of pats on the back. Before long I found my self in the living room, where I found Audrie, Dalton's wife, and she had questions. I answered her with only nods and shakes of my head. This uncharacteristic silence had her concerned and she called my mother over so they could investigate.

"Why won't Thomas say anything?" Audrie asked my mom.

"That is strange, now I think about it he has been quiet all day." Mom said with intrigue. "Come over here," mom said with force. "Say something." She demanded.

I just shook my head, no.

Her eyes got angry "Say something!" she demanded again.

I shook my head no, again.

"Do you have something in your mouth?" she asked.

I shrugged my shoulders, and raised my eyebrows, still not saying anything.

"What do you have in your mouth," she said grabbing my cheeks to break the silent seal. "Give it to me."

"Ow, get off me." I said, struggling against her grip on my cheeks and pulled back from her.

Moms and Audrie's eyes grew large, their mouths opened with shock.

I had gotten up early that morning. I liked to be the first one up. That way I could raid the fridge for chocolate, and no one could stop me. I found my plastic cup and filled it with a handful of chocolate chips, then went over to the sofa and enjoyed my predawn snack. I finished the bitter chocolate quickly and went back for more. I opened the fridge and got another handful of the chocolate chips. Then I wondered if mom had anymore treats used for baking hidden in the cupboard. I pulled over a chair and investigated the baking supplies within.

Mom always made colorful cookies, and they were delicious, so when I found the food coloring I wondered if it was the source of the flavor. I pulled the first bottle out and popped the yellow cap. Letting a few drops fall onto my tongue. There was no flavor at all, so I returned the cap and put it back in its place. Yellow was boring, why would it have any flavor. I pulled out the next bottle, and popped the cap wondering what flavor is blue. With the disappointment of the yellow, I gave the blue bottle a good squeeze. The blue tasted the same as the yellow, like nothing at all. So, I returned the bottle back to the cupboard and abandoned the quest for different baking treats. I slid the chair back to the table and went back to the sofa to enjoy the second handful of chocolate chips.

As the house began to wake up, I went into the bathroom to use it before the others. As I passed the mirror, I gave myself a toothy grin. My eyes blinked back from my reflection, trying to make sense of my blue tongue, teeth and gums. I pulled out my toothbrush and scrubbed my teeth. The blue didn't even fade. Oh no, I wasn't going to be able to hide this for long. I rinsed out my mouth, the water fell from my face, clear. I was going to be stuck like this for the whole day for sure. So, I just decided to keep my mouth shut, if nobody noticed, I wouldn't have to get in trouble for eating the chocolate chips.

I had made it most of the day, until mom had pinched my cheeks. Until then I was doing well at keeping the secret.

Moms and Audrie's eyes grew large at the shock of seeing me with blue teeth. I pushed moms' hand away, and they started to laugh. Mom instantly knew what I had ingested and shook her head in disbelief.

"We should use the food coloring every day, if it keeps him this quiet." Mom joked with Audrie who giggled at the idea.

"Not funny," I said, my forehead wrinkling with disapproval.

Now that the truth was out about my blue teeth I went back and visited with the old people in the kitchen, waiting for the party cake and ice-cream.

Apple Sauce

Mom and dad had gone out of town for a conference or a trade show, I didn't know the difference. Dad had a few opportunities each year to take mom with him when he traveled for work. It must have been somewhere warm, because mom was excited to go.

Grandma Eva was going to stay over and look after my sister and I while they were away for a few days. This was going to be great. Grandma was always fun when she visited. We would complete puzzles, draw in coloring books and play cards for hours.

Sitting at the kitchen table the three of us used new crayons to color in our coloring books. Grandmas' pictures always turned out beautifully. She would put a dark colored outline around the picture then color in the center with the same color, only lighter. It gave her finished pictures the illusion of glowing, and she used this technique on every page. I was around six years old; my sister Lisa was four. I was mischievous and my little sister was my shadow. When we finished our coloring pages Grandma asked what we would like for dinner.

"Apple sauce." I quickly replied

"Yea, apple sauce," my sister quickly parroted.

"You kids sure like apple sauce," she said. "But ok, if that's what you want."

My sister and I nodded like idiots, confirming our dinner request. Grandma got up from the table to prepare some pork chops with apple sauce. This was the same meal she had prepared for the last three nights. Every time she would ask us about dinner, we would just say apple sauce. Except for breakfast, then we would ask her to make apple pancakes. Nobody makes better apple pancakes than Grandma, nobody!

My parents returned home from their adventures the next day late in the afternoon. Mom was barely in the door before she asked Grandma for a situation report on our behavior, as we could be a handful.

Grandma thought about it for a moment and said, "they were behaved, but they sure love apple sauce."

Mom laughed "apple sauce, I'm sure the do." She said sarcastically.

Grandma not catching the tone continued "yea, I made it for them every night, that's all they wanted to eat."

"Oh grandma, those kids played a trick on you." Mom explained. "We always use the word apple sauce to mean nothing." Giving grandma an example.

"Were you always busy playing cards or working on the coloring books?" mom asked.

Grandma nodded.

"So, when you asked them to take a break, or have an interruption for dinner, they would just say apple sauce, right?" mom asked again.

"Yes, how did you know?" Grandma asked.

"Apple sauce means nothing, as they wanted to just continue doing whatever fun thing you were all working on." Mom said with a big smile. "Who has time to eat when your spending quality time with grandma playing cards."

"Not us," I said

"Yea, not us," my sister copied.

Grandma looked over at us, sitting at the table. "Oh, you kids sure tricked old granny with your apple sauce." She smiled big and we all had a good chuckle.

Lost Shoe Trouble

I had been called home for dinner. We were a family that had dinner every night at the same time. I was playing across the street at Nick's house and had lost track of time. My grandma had called over to his house and asked his mom to send me on my way. My parents were away on another working vacation, and I was pushing all the boundaries. Nick's mom told me it was time to go home, so I put my shoes on at the back door and started home. I knew that I would be back in an hour anyway. We lived right across the street from one another and dinner was only a minor inconvenience.

I ran along the side of the house, pushing the tall white gate open at the end of the sidewalk. I rushed across the front yard and stopped on the sidewalk, looking both ways before I crossed over the road. The street was empty, and I started across.

I'm sitting on the street next to the truck that is parked in front of the neighbor's house. My back is against the trucks front tire and I'm on the ground. I look around to see where I am. A man is approaching me, someone I don't know.

"Hey, kid," he starts to say, as I spring to my feet.

As soon as I was standing, I ran home. I'm late for dinner after all. I ran up the patio stones that approached our front door, following them around to the side of the house. Rushing into the house through the unlocked back door. I looked down at my socks, wondering hey where are my shoes. Grandma was in the front room waiting, so I went to sit in there with her. I sat in the round chair with the flowered rose pattern. The moment I was seated in the chair the doorbell rang. Grandma got up off the long sofa with the same flowered pattern to answer the front door.

Standing on the front step was the man I had seen on the street. Grandma opened the inside door, leaving the screen door closed.

"Hello, can I help you?" she asked.

"Hi, um, I think I hit your kid with my car." The man said cautiously, not wanting to raise any unnecessary alarm. "I saw him run into your backyard."

I was sitting in the chair directly behind my grandma and was blocked from his view. I pressed my back firmly into the chair, the pressure was comforting. Grandma took a step back and looked over at me.

"Did you get hit by a car?" she asked with great concern on her face.

"Nope, wasn't me." I said as I pressed deeper into the chair.

The man on the step was now able to see into the house and could see me on the chair. "That's the boy." He said, pointing from outside the door.

"Nope, wasn't me." I said as I pressing even deeper into the chair.

"I have his shoes," the man said as he held out my still laced up shoes.

Grandma looked over at me with panic in her eyes. "Why are you sitting like that?" she asked. "And why does he have your shoes?

Grandma stepped over to me and pulled me forward in the chair. I tried to make an objection but before I could, she was pulling up the back of my shirt. My shirt was covered with dirt and small rocks from the road. She let out a gasp as she looked at my back. I was scratched up and bleeding slightly.

"Were you hit by a car?" she asked again with a tremble in her voice, tired of my evasion.

"I don't know, maybe." I said still not completely sure of what had happened.

"I didn't see him in the road, until he was up in the air," The man on the step said. "I knocked him right out of his shoes," he said shocked. "When I went to see if he was ok, he got up and ran away, but I have his shoes." The man explained, extending the shoes out again.

Grandma opened the screen door and took my shoes back from the man. Seeing that I was not dead or dying, he turned around and left. Grandma then turned her full attention to me. Pulling off my shirt to get a good look at my damaged body.

She raised my arms and asked, "does anything hurt?"

"Um, no," I said. Taking a moment to calm myself as the adrenaline was starting to subside and my hands started to tremble. "I don't think so."

"Don't move, wait here." Grandma demanded as she rushed out the front door and raced over to the neighbor's house.

She was back in a flash with the neighbour.

"We need to go to the clinic, you need to be checked over, just to make sure everything is ok." She explained as she pushed me forward in the chair, allowing the neighbor to have a quick look at my hit by a car injuries.

I was getting cold as my body started to go into shock, I reached over and grabbed my dirty shirt and put it back on. Grandma hastily put on my returned, still tied shoes, and we left the house for the clinic.

I don't remember much about the clinic, other than it was a big brick building with a large round window.

We returned home after the quick inspection from the doctor. Nothing was broken, just a few scrapes. Once we were home and safe, I was interrogated as to why I didn't say anything about the accident.

Grandma started in "why did you not tell us you were hit by a car?"

"I don't know, I didn't want to get in trouble," I said. Knowing there was trouble to be had, and that I didn't want any of it.

Grandma coddled me with "Oh sweetie, you weren't in any trouble." "We were just scared that you got hurt." "Getting hit by a car is serious."

I smiled up at her repeating something my dad always says, "Don't worry Grandma, you can't hurt steel."

She smiled back and shook her head "let's go get something to eat, I'm sure you're starving." "What do you want?" she asked.

I grinned big and answered, "apple sauce."

Thomas Ncamtu

The Trouble with Third Grade

I have always been kind of block head. I was born stubborn like my father and my grandfather, probably like every one of our family from the beginning of time. School was the place where authority tried to force me to conform to the rules, and I was having none of it. I was a good kid, quick to help or volunteer, but I was not a good student. I was set in my ways and was not going to change without a fight.

The problem started with a math test. It was easy enough, simple addition and subtraction. I went down the list of twenty questions. Two plus one, three, I wrote the answer with confidence. One plus two, three, I refused to write the answer and moved on. Three plus four, seven, I wrote the answer. Four plus three, seven, I skipped writing the second answer and moved on to the next question. I got to the bottom of the page, satisfied with the answers provided, and took the test up to the teachers' desk for her review.

She took the page and looked it over. Making quick marks with her bright red pen. She put some extra gusto into the answers I didn't fill in, making large crosses on the page.

"Why didn't you answer these questions? She asked. "You knew the answers, you got them right on the questions before," she looked down at me with disapproving eyebrows.

"I know that the answer is the same for both questions," I explained. "The numbers are just in opposite positions." "So, if they are the same, I'm not doing it twice." I said with my childish confidence.

"You have to fill in all the answers, that's what the test is about." She explained. "To show that you know the answers."

I wasn't having any of it. I stood firm on my refusal to do the same thing twice and told her why.

"If I know the answers are the same for every other question, and you know that I know the answers, what's the problem?" I said starting to give some attitude.

She scowled back at me with a visceral distain for me not blindly accepting her authority.

"That's not the point, you need to write it down for them to count." Her voice beginning to raise.

"Well, I'm not going to do it." I said loudly.

Refusing to give into the redundancy of the questions. Our elevated voices were starting to get the attention of the other kids in the classroom.

"You will do what your told, and if not, you can sit in the hallway." She barked loudly as a warning to the other children not to step out of line.

She grabbed me firmly by the arm and pulled me towards the door. Her tight grip pinching my skin as I was pushed out into the hallway. She pointed at a desk that was already in the hall.

"Sit there and don't move until you are ready to follow instructions." She said firmly.

She moved back into the classroom and closed the door with an unintended level of force, making a loud bang as it slammed shut.

I sat in the desk and enjoyed the silence of the hallway. If this was going to be a battle of wills, I would be victorious, I had generations of blockheads cheering me on. I opened the wooden desktop to see if there were any interesting things forgotten inside. The desk was empty, so I just sat there, in silence, waiting for the end of the day.

When I got home from school mom asked, "How was your day?" as I walked into the kitchen.

"I got to look at books all day," I said not mentioning the disagreement I had with the teacher over the math test.

"That's, good," mom said as she went back to making something wonderful for dinner.

The next day I went into the classroom and was immediately confronted by the teacher.

"Are you going to answer all of the math questions today?" she asked with a triumphant tone, thinking she had won the battle of wills.

The smile quickly fell from her lips when with my insubordination told her, "Nope, I won't answer the same question twice."

Before I could finish my thought, her hand was around my arm, and I was back out in the hallway sitting alone in the same desk as the day before.

"You will stay there until your ready to cooperate," she said, turning to go back into the classroom, not waiting for my retort.

I looked up from the desk, squinting across the hall to the bookshelf that I had spent the previous day staring at. I got up and chose a book quickly. Returning to my seat with a book about animals, getting back in position before the teacher noticed I was out of the desk. There was no need to waist the whole day not being entertained.

When I got home from school that day mom asked, "How was your day?" The same way she always asked.

"I got to look at books all day," I said, still not mentioning the disagreement I had with the teacher the day before.

Mom looked over at me with a quizzical expression and I knew I was going to have some explaining to do.

"What do you mean by that." She enquired. "Did you read books all day again?" she pried.

"No, I didn't read any books today. I just sat in my desk and looked at the books." "Just like the teacher told me too." I explained to my mother in a way that wouldn't garner too much attention.

But you can't fool her, she knew something was going on.

"That sounds nice," she said making me think I was clever with my half truth. "I'm going to school with you tomorrow to see all these books you have not been reading." Before I could even make an objection, she finished with, "and have a word with that teacher about what has been going on."

The next morning mom and I walked to school. I wasn't worried about getting into any type of trouble, I thought I was on the right side of the argument. We went into the school and started towards the classroom. Mom would occasionally volunteer at the school and stopped to chat with one of the other teachers. I went into the classroom and tried to sit in my regular desk. I was confronted by the teacher before I even had a chance to warm the seat.

"Are you going to answer all the math questions today?" she asked with an angry tone, knowing that I was not going to obey her yet again.

"Nope." I said firmly with a big grin spread across my face.

She grabbed me by my arm and pulled me across the classroom straight out into the hallway. We had just stepped off the carpet onto the grey tiles of the hall when my mother was walking up to the door.

"Hey! What the hell is going on here!" Mom asked with an elevated voice. "Take you hands off my kid!"

Mom using the detective skills all mothers have, quickly figured out what was going on. Her eyes rested for a quick moment on the desk in the hallway, then over to the bookshelf on the other side of the hall that it faced. She knew what was going on. Her eyes shot back over to the teacher with a burning gaze. The teacher was struggling to find the words to explain what had just happened.

Without breaking eye contact with the teacher, my mom asked me "Are those the books you have been looking at for the last couple of days."

"Yes," I answered quickly not wanting her to look in my direction.

"Go sit in the classroom, I need a word with your teacher." Mom instructed.

I moved quickly back to the desk in the classroom. I could see mom and the teacher talking in the doorway. I couldn't hear the conversation, but mom was unnecessarily close to the teacher, and her hands were quite animated. After a few moments mom waived from the door.

"Enjoy the rest of the day Thomas, see you after school." Mom said with a wink.

I knew I was going to have a hard conversation when I got home. But for now, I was back in the classroom where I belonged. The teacher scurred behind her desk and taught the lessons. Her gaze never looking in my direction for the whole day.

When I got home from school that day mom asked, "How was your day?" The same way she always asked, everyday.

But before I could answer she began with the interrogation.

"I had a quick chat with your teacher about you not finishing a math test?" mom asked as a question.

My mother knew all the excuses I was about to make up, but wanted to see how our two stories would match up.

"Yea, I had a math test on Monday." I explained. "I knew all the answers." I said, taking a moment to figure out how to speak about my refusal to do the work. "They tried to trick us by having the number flipped around, but the answers were the same, so I wasn't fooled and just skipped over them." I said confidently.

Mom looked over at me with a smile, impressed by my mental gymnastics and said "Well, next time, even if they are trying to trick you, fill in all the answers anyway." "I don't want you to give that poor teacher any more trouble." Mom continued "you might cause her head to pop off," Mom said in her most diplomatic tone. "I don't want you to spend anymore time in that hallway either, so if you do, let me know, right away." Mom smiled again, "so I can have another talk with the teacher." She finished, half as a warning to me and half as reassurance that she had my back. "Understand?" she said firmly.

I nodded with understanding and rushed out of the room, happy that the incident didn't need to be escalated into any form of at home punishment.

I finished out that school year without anymore fieldtrips to the hallway. The teacher did her best not to have any contact with me at all, we both just coexisted in the classroom and that was fine with me.

On my next math test I did reluctantly fill out the questions that were designed to trick me with redundancy of the same answers.

Scavenger Hunt

I have always loved to find treasures. I wasn't allowed to go to far from home, so my search area was limited. I would wander down the alley looking for things that were out of place and might have some value for future use. The house next to Daltons was owned by an old lady we called Grandma Mary. She was super old and always smelled of cigarettes. As I exited the gate onto the gravel I noticed some new boxes on the side of her garage. They were on the other side of the short once painted white fence.

The boxes were bursting at the seams with green Christmas garland and other holiday trinkets. I rushed over, climbing the short fence, and opened the boxes to have a good look inside. What I found would be perfect for decorating the playhouse. The box was too deep for me to pickup with my short arms, so I just took what I could carry. Planning on making multiple visits to empty the boxes. After an hour and ten trips, I had emptied the contents of the boxes. There had been all sorts of discarded Christmas decorations in the boxes, and now I had them spread out all over the grass in front of the playhouse.

I called into the house to get my sister, so she could help me decorate. She was excited to see all the new treasures and rushed outside to get started.

When my dad built us the playhouse, he used as a simple design. Four square walls and a raised floor. Then a peaked roof that was attached as a separate piece. It was built like a cookie jar. The roof of the playhouse was shingled with the same shingles as the house from the leftovers when the houses' roof was redone. There was a rectangular door that was just slightly taller than I was, but not much wider. Windows were cutout of the walls on the front and left side. The left window had a great view of the fence. The whole structure was painted a cream color then accented with dads' favorite color burgundy. The window frames and door trim were the rusty red. The finished project matched the house perfectly. We were lucky to have the back yard shelter and spent most afternoons inside.

We started to hang the green garland and tree lights around the inside of the small room, draping the foil through the roof joists. I stood on a small stool to reach the high spots. Before we knew it the place was a festive wonder. I placed any unbroken bobbles along the hanging garland and disposed of anything that were broken. By time we were finished decorating it was almost lunch. Mom called us in for a quick soup and a sandwich just as the final touches were being made.

"What are you two working on out there?" mom asked, as she flipped the grilled cheese sandwich in the pan. "It sure is quiet out there, are you keeping out of trouble?"

My sister answered excitedly "Were decorating the playhouse for Christmas!" "Thomas got some decorations."

"What did you find this time?" mom asked half annoyed.

I was always coming back with all kinds of junk.

"I got some Christmas stuff from Grandma Mary." I explained. "it's perfect for the playhouse." Purposely leaving out the fact that it was found in her garbage area.

After lunch my sister and I rushed back outside to show mom the festive abomination we had created.

We got around the corner of the house and stopped dead in our tracks. The stink that was emanating from the playhouse was thick and nauseating. Years of cigarette smoke must have been released as we unravelled all the Christmas treasures.

Mom stood back and looked at our work. "Well, it sure does look good, and you two did a nice job, but that smell is terrible."

Mom wasn't wrong the smell was gag inducing bad.

"I'll go get a garbage bag and you two can take it down a put it back in the garbage," mom said as my sister, and I nodded in agreement.

We spent the rest of the afternoon taking down the decorations and returned them to the garbage. The smell stuck to our hands and lingered for days. No matter how many times they were washed the stink would just not leave. The playhouse took weeks before the smell had permanently disappeared. It was fun to decorate the playhouse but the Christmas abomination we created wasn't worth all the smelly effort.

Rubber Band Launch

The next week I was back at my treasure hunt. I had wandered a few houses further than I would normally go and found a fantastic treasure. On this excursion I found the biggest rubber band I have ever seen. It was an inch wide and five feet long. I don't know what it would have been originally used for, but it was mine now and I had a few bad ideas. The rubber band was still flexible and in one piece, so the possibilities were endless. (Did you roll your eyes, I did, couldn't help myself.)

I returned home and dropped the rubber band in the backyard. I rushed across the street, making sure to look both ways before crossing. I was excited to show Nick my new find. I told him of the treasure then we both returned to the yard. I showed him the giant rubber band and he was amazed. He thought I had been exaggerating its massive size.

We decided it would be fun to launch our action figure with it. We hooked one side of the band around the top of the fence, the other to the branch of the dead tree that was in the middle of the yard. The rubber band reached both points with ease. There was still some slack in the rubber band as it rested between the tree and the fence.

We took turns putting our figures in the giant sling shot. With the figure held in place I would take ten big steps backwards, pulling for the most tension as possible. Sending the plastic man flying across the yard as the rubber returned to its original position. The plastic figures would tumble and spin as they launched through the air. We took turns and launched the characters dozens of times before disaster struck.

Nick was out in the grass retrieving his last tossed figure, I was setting up for my next turn. I had the band stretched out before Nick was fully out of the way and lost my grip on the rubber. The rubber band shot forward and smacked Nick right across the back.

The bellow that he emitted was primal screech. It wasn't a cry or a scream but something from deep within his guts. The rubber whipped the air out of his lungs, and he was unable to speak. The horrible noise that he made rippled across the neighborhood and his mother had come a running to see what had happened. His mom was in the yard with a flash to check on the state of her boy. Nick was standing, marching around speechless with his hands on his back, still unable to speak anything more than a single syllable at a time.

"We were playing with the rubber band," I explained "and he got smacked in the back."

She rushed over to him, and he started to get composed enough to tell her the same story. Nick explained it was an accident, and he that was going to live. She lifted his shirt to see the damage caused by the stinging rubber. His mom let out a gasp as she investigated the injury. His back had a two-inch white line running across the bottom of his shoulder blades. Three inches above and below the white line the skin was already purple. Nick had bruised quickly, and his mother was pissed.

"This thing is going in the garbage," she said as she pulled the rubber band off the tree. "Its dangerous, and it's gone."

I didn't even try to make an objection after seeing Nicks back. I don't think we would have played with the rubber band again anyway it was dangerous. She took the rubber band off the fence and escorted Nick back home to tend to his slapping elastic wounds. I followed them out of the back yard making my apologies for the pain that I had caused. Making sure that Nick would survive so we could paly again the next day, promising to find new ways to get into trouble and not get hurt.

Now That's a Treasure

Two houses down the street lived Luke and Melissa. We were all around the same age and played in the yards together. My sister and I would spend time over at their house watching movies. Their mom made the best popcorn, it was buttered and seasoned to perfection. We would all share from a giant wooden bowl while we watched parent approved movies. I remember watching the Ewok movie at Luke's house, the giant monster terrified me for weeks.

I would have been considered a bad influence on Luke. His house had more religious rules than ours did. We both had our He-man action figures; I had some heroes and some villains. My imaginary battles for the universe were epic tales of good vs. evil. Luke was only allowed to have the heroes. His imaginary battles would consist of a strong disagreement over a tea party.

One day while I was on a treasure hunt, I found the holy grail of epic finds. I collected the box and returned its contents back to the playhouse. I was excited to share my find and rushed over to Lukes's house to get him. I rang the doorbell, and his mom answered.

"Can Luke come out and play?" I asked.

"Luke, Thomas is here, go out and play." She called into the house.

Luke arrived quickly with his shoes in hand, cutting his universal tea party short, and we rushed out the door.

"you kids be good," his mom shouted, as we ran across the grass back towards my house.

"You will never guess what I found," I teased Luke.

"What?" he said with some scepticism.

He wasn't always impressed by the junk I found.

"I have them hiding in the playhouse, lets go." I said with a grin.

"Sure, lets go." He repeated unsure of what awaited him.

We went in the back yard and into the playhouse. We sat at the small table and chairs that filled most of the back corner of the small room. I had the box hidden under the table. I reached into the box and pulled out a magazine and handed it to Luke. His eyes popped out of his head, just like one of his bug-eyed action figures.

On my treasure hunt that day I had found a file box of discarded nudie magazines; and it was the best day ever! Luke and I sat at the small table and flipped through the glossy pages. We were getting our first female anatomy lesson that day and it was glorious. Dinner time arrived way to soon and it was time for Luke to go home for supper.

"Can I take this with me?" Luke asked.

"Sure, why not I have a whole box of them," I said, handing him a second one.

"Thanks," Luke said taking the magazines, "I have to get home, see you tomorrow."

"Yea, I better go eat too." I said, "see you later."

Luke left for home, and I put my magazine back in the box, adjusting the lid back into place. I pushed the box back under the table, then I went into the house for dinner.

We were about halfway through eating dinner when there was a frantic knock on the front door. Mom got up from the table to see who was making all the noise. It was Luke's mom, and she was pissed. My mom had only opened the screen door a crack before Luke's mom burst into the house and started her tirade.

"Look what my son brought home." She harped, waiving the magazine in her one hand. "Look at this disgusting filth."

Mom took a moment to try and catch a glimpse of the flailing pages in her hysterical hands.

"What is it?" mom asked firmly, reaching out to grab the magazine.

It only took my mom a second to recognize the text on the front cover to know what the problem was.

"Look at this garbage." Lukes's mom went on. "My precious Luke has been tainted and it's Thomas' fault."

Mom called into the kitchen for me to come to the front door and confront the allegations. "Did you give this to Luke? She asked.

"What?" I asked quickly. Following rule number one of being a boy, deny everything, always.

I was not going to admit to anything until I was cornered and there were no ways to escape.

"Did you give Luke this nudie magazine" mom began to interrogate me.

"I don't know, let me have a look." I said reaching for the magazine, knowing it was going to be the last time I would see some glossy boobies for a while.

"I don't think so," mom said pulling the magazine out of my reach.

Lukes's mom was going crazy "Luke told me everything, Thomas has a whole box of this smut in that tiny house in the back yard."

"Is that true?" mom asked concerned. "Well let's go get them," she said, her anger starting to show. "Where did you even get these from?" she grilled.

Six Lives Left

I knew that if mom went into the playhouse, she would find them all under the table, so it was time to come clean.

"I found them on a treasure hunt today." I explained. "Luke and I were looking at them this afternoon and he took one home." "We were reading them for the articles and never even noticed the naked ladies." I said with a big grin.

"See, I told you he corrupted my boy!" Luke's mom barked.

"Yes, yes, I see your point, but I'm sure its not quite that bad, boys will be boys." Mom tried to calm the situation. "I will make sure that all of these books of the devil get put back in the trash."

This promise seemed to calm down Lukes's mom enough that she went back home. After dinner mom went outside and confiscated the box of nudity and returned it to the trash. Another word was never spoken about it.

Luke wasn't as dumb as he looked, his mom only had one magazine when she stormed over. He must have hidden the other before she could take it away. I don't know what happened with that, I never saw that second magazine ever again.

The Story of Boots

Our neighbor Karl got a new puppy and named him Boots. Boots was a cocker spaniel. I could see his tiny body through the space between fence boards, as he ran around the neighbor's yard. I was excited to get over there and play with the rambunctious little pup. Karl must have seen my eyes peering through the space between the boards and called over to me.

"Hey, do you want to come play with Boots?" Karl asked with a big smile.

"I, sure do." I said with excitement as I started to climb the fence, not needing to be asked twice.

Our side of the fence had the cross boards and that made for an easy climb over the white fence. I got over the fence in record time. I made sure not to land on the dog when I jumped off the top board onto the grass. Boots immediately ran over and greeted me with a juicy dog kiss. His golden fur was soft when I ran my fingers down his back. The dog bounced and hopped with excitement at the new attention. Boots was tied to a long tether to keep him in the yard. The rope and collar hung loosely around his neck, giving him almost enough rope to explore the whole yard.

"What kind of dog is it?" I asked. Not that it mattered to me, I only new dogs by their sizes, and Boots was small and cute.

"Boots is a cocker spaniel," Karl said.

"How big is he going to grow?" I asked, scratching behind the dog's floppy ears.

"Not too much bigger, he will maybe come up to your knees when he is full grown." Karl explained. "Well, I have some stuff to do inside, you can stay and play with the dog as long as you want."

"Thanks, I will stay here for a bit." I said, as Karl turned and went inside the house.

I sat on the ground near the back door of the house and played with the dog. When boots had his fill of belly rubs, he ran off to get his ball. The green tennis ball was delivered at my feet, with the expectation of me to giving it a toss back into the yard. I picked up the wet juicy ball and gave it a light throw. The ball bounced and rolled into the grass; Boots was in quick pursuit. He grabbed the ball and made a hasty return, eager to play some more. I pulled at the ball; He refused to give it up without a struggle. We played a tug of war until his small jaw released the ball, and it was dripping in my hand. I tossed the slimy ball back into the yard again. Boots was fast to retrieve it again, and ran back to me quickly, so I could throw it again.

I must have tossed the ball twenty times and decided it was almost time to go home for some lunch. I stood up and boots dropped the ball at my feet, wanting to play more.

"This is the last toss; I have to go for lunch." I negotiated with the big-eyed puppy.

I lobbed the ball into the yard, it landed on the grass and rolled. Boots chased after it at full speed. The ball had rolled just outside the range that the tether would allow. The rope went taught, and Boots was unexpectedly stopped in his tracks. With the ball was just out of his reach, his small body did a forced U-turn from the force of the rope. Boots was surprised and shocked by the sudden pain he felt and turned his attention back to me.

With revenge in his eye's Boots charged over to me. When he was within range he pounced and knocked me down. I fell onto the grass and was surprised by the sudden change in the dogs deminer. I didn't mean to toss the ball so far, but Boots was hurting, and I was the cause of his discomfort. The small dog sat on my chest, barking his warning inches away from my unblinking eyes.

Karl rushed out to find the dog on top of me and quickly pushed him off. We had been playing for over a half hour and the dog hadn't made a single growl, let alone a bark. So, Karl was concerned when he had heard the dog's angry barks. I looked up at Karl and he had a look of fear in his eyes.

"Yvonne, get over here quick." He yelled, calling over to my mother.

Karls deep voice boomed. The neighborhood was normally quiet and his voice caried into the house alerting my mother of the situation.

Mom came running over to the fence, looking over to see what the problem was.

"What's going on?" she asked concerned by the sudden disruption to the piece and quiet.

Peeking over the fence she looked down on me, laying on the ground, my face covered in blood. Mom moved quickly around the fence to the gate. She nearly crashed into Dalton as they both tried to enter Karl's yard at the same time. Dalton had heard the bellow Karl had produced, and didn't like the tone, Dalton, guessing something was wrong, rushed over to investigate. Mom and Dalton arrived by my side, both concerned about my bloodied condition.

"What happened?" mom asked.

"Thomas was playing with Boots, and when I came outside the dog was on top of him!" Karl explained the situation as best he could.

I Looked up from the ground, not knowing what the problem was. I was just knocked over by the dog. No big deal. But all the adults were clearly agitated. I reached up to my face and rubbed an itch near my left eye, my hand returned bloodied.

"He got bit by the dog." Dalton said, assessing the situation quickly, as he scooped me off the ground. "We better go to the clinic; he probably needs stitches." He exclaimed.

"Let me go grab my purse and I will meet you at the car" mom said, rushing home to get the paperwork needed for our almost habitual clinic visit.

Dalton took me to his vehicle and put me in the backseat. He grabbed some paper towels from the work bench.

"Hold this over your eye," he told me. "Try not to get blood all over the car." Dalton said with a cheeky smile.

I still didn't know what the fuss was about, but everyone was rushing around. Mom was back to the vehicle, ready to go in mere moments. Boots was sitting in the yard, looking small and remorseful, as we drove off to the clinic.

Once I was looked over by the doctor the damage was revealed. I had a small cut on my lip and a tiny divot by my left eye. The damage was minimal, but all the blood made it look worse than it was. When boots knocked me over his sharp puppy claws must have scratched into my face and done the accidental damage. I didn't think it was that big of a deal, and chicks dig scars. I went home with a couple of Band-Aids on my face and a dog attack story to exaggerate to my father.

When we got home Boots was gone. He was returned to wherever Karl had got him from in the first place. I was disappointed because I wanted to watch that little puppy grow up. It was an accident on both sides. I didn't mean to throw the ball that far and I'm sure he didn't mean to draw blood. I don't know where Boots went but I'm sure he ended up in a good home with no more yard tethers.

The next week when I was on my treasure hunt, I found a dog of my own to bring home. I had wandered further than I normally did, when I was approached by a giant hound dog with his tail wagging. I had no fear as the monstrous beast greeted me with a sloppy kiss. I draped my arm around his tall neck and began the journey home. I had made a new dog friend and was excited to introduce them to the family. I opened the back gate, and mom was working in the yard. Her eyes bugged out of her head when she saw the two of us come through the gate.

"Can we keep him mom?" I asked with excited intentions.

"No, we can't keep him!" mom said sternly. "Where did you even find such a beast. Your lucky he didn't eat you in one bite." She scolded me, still shaken by the last dog incident.

"But mom," I said and before I could even plead my case she interjected.

"No, we need to take him back to his house." She said. "His owners are probably worried." "If you lost your dog, you would be sad right?" she negotiated. "Then we should get him home right, lets go."

Before I had a chance to weight the options, the three of us were turned around and walking back out the gate towards where I had first captured the friendly animal.

We had gotten to just about to where I first met the giant dog, and a lady was walking out of her yard. She looked frantic and upon seeing us coming down the lane, walking in her direction with the giant beast, her tension lifted from her shoulders.

"Oh, thank goodness." She said, "you found him," Referring to my new friend. "He must has snuck out the gate."

I let go of the dog's collar and he trotted over to her and licked her hand. "Thank you for bring him home," she said. "He likes to take himself for a walk every now and then." She explained with a big smile.

I mustered a "you're welcome," and waved goodbye to the big dog and his owner.

Mom and I turned to walk back home dogless.

"See, don't you feel better knowing that the dog has a good home." Mom said. I didn't respond. "I was surprised to see you with such a big animal, especially after what happen with boots." "Were you not scared that he was going to eat you?" Mom leaned in and grabbed my belly for added effect.

"No, I wasn't scared," I laughed. As we continued home, dogless.

The Neighbor of Mr. Rogers

Corra Penner lived next to Mr. Rogers. I passed her house every day on the way to school. It was a nice-looking house with dark bricks framed around the front door. Corra would come out of her house and run across the street, so we could walk to school together. At the end of each day, I would walk with her back home. We had been walking to school together for awhile and one day on the way home she asked me to come inside.

"Do you want to come meet my dog." Corra asked with a smile. "His name is Rusty," she said with excitement.

"Of course I do, I like dogs." I said, still fearless from my encounter with boots.

"Great, Grandma probably made some cookies too." She said. Grabbing my hand as we crossed the street towards her front yard.

We walked up the front steps and went into the house. All houses looked the same on the inside, but it reminded me of my grandparent's house in Regina. We were greeted by her grandma before the door even had a chance to close behind us.

"Hey sweetie how was school? Grandma asked Corra, "who is your friend."

"School was good grandma, this is Thomas." Corra explained, "I brought him over so he could meet Rusty."

"Ok, I will let Rusty inside in a few minutes." Her grandma said. "Go sit on the sofa and I will bring you kids some fresh baked cookies."

The house smelled of the fresh baking, reminding me of when mom made her cookies. We went into the living room and sat on the flower-patterned sofa. The tv in the corner was turned on and was playing Mary Poppins.

"Have you ever seen this movie before?" Corra asked.

I took a moment to look at the screen and watched a few seconds of singing and dancing and replied "No, I don't think I have."

"It's one of my favorites." Corra said with a cute smile.

Her grandma returned with a plate full of fresh chocolate chip cookies. Granda extended the plate, and I took my time to select the best-looking cookie. They were all big, and the chocolate chips were abundant, so I just took the one on top.

"Thank you" I said. "Chocolate chip cookies are my favorite."

"You're very welcome," she said. "I'm going to go let Rusty back in the house."

Corra took her oversized cookie from the plate before grandma went to let the dog inside. I was almost finished my delicious cookie when the dog ran into the living room. It stopped in the middle of the room and stared at Corra and I. It barked a single time and approached the sofa.

"This is Rusty," Corra said as she gave scratches to the top his head. "Don't worry he doesn't bite, much." She laughed, trying to make me do the same.

"I'm not scared of dogs," I said as I reached out to touch his soft fur, "what kind of dog is he?"

"Rusty is a collie, just like Lassie" Corra explained. "Do you want to see his trick?" she said with a sneaky smile.

"Sure, I like tricks." I said, not knowing what she had planned, expecting him to roll over or play dead.

"So, if you put your arm out like this, he will do it." She explained. She held her arm out in front of her, bent at the elbow and out across her chest. Rusty's tail was wagging with excitement ready to show off his secret skills. She dropped her arm quickly before he could preform the trick.

"Now you do it." She pushed, not wanting to ruin the surprise. "But hold still."

I bent my arm and held it out in front of my chest. Rusty approached and quickly clamped his jaw onto my arm. My eyes got big, and I didn't dare move a single muscle or make a sound. I could feel his teeth on my skin, and his slobber running down my arm. The dogs' tongue was warm as it licked my forearm.

"Oh good, Rusty likes you," Grandam said as she entered the room. "If he didn't you would have a bloody stump where your arm was."

They both laughed as my eyes got even bigger. Rusty held on for a few more seconds, then let go of my slobbered arm. His tail was wagging furiously as he waited for his positive reinforcement.

"Good boy, Rusty" Corra said as she reached out to scratched under his chin.

We sat around for a while, talking about nothing, before I noticed the time. I was going to be late for dinner and had to go home. I still had a block and a half to go before I would arrive in my yard.

"Thank you again for the delicious cookies" I said. As I went towards the door to put on my shoes.

Corra walked me over to the door and planted a quick kiss on my surprised lips. "See you tomorrow." She said blushing.

"See you tomorrow," I repeated feeling the heat in my face start to rise. I left the house and made it home with haste. My feet not touching the sideway as I floated home. That was my first kiss, and it was glorious, even if I did have dog slobber running down my arm.

Six Lives Left

The next few weeks Corra and I walk together to school holding hands. It was a nice couple of weeks. We would laugh and joke as we wandered the block to school. It was a short-lived romance, as my family and I were moving across town at the end of the school year, but we were happy for those few short weeks.

Thomas Neamtu

Teaching Ducks to Fly

On Saturday afternoon I wandered over to Nicks house. I rang the doorbell; his mother answered and directed me to the back yard. I went around the side of the house and opened the white wooden gate. The gate swung closed behind me quickly, the tension on the spring must have just been adjusted, as the slamming gate surprised me. I found Nick in the back yard looking into a cardboard box. The box was large, and I rushed over to peek inside, excited to see his new treasure.

Inside the box were five baby ducks. The ducklings did not have any feathers and were still fluffy. They were extremely cute as the frolicked inside the box, trying to get out. Nick and I investigated the box for a few minutes, before his dad showed up and stood next to us in the yard.

"If your gentle, you can pick one up." He said to the both of us.

Nick reached in and selected his fluffy yellow duckling, then I reached in for mine. The duck's body was surprisingly light. The fluff was so soft. I could feel the heartbeat throb in between my hands. The tiny bird made a small, adorable squawk but didn't wiggle between my fingers. We held the birds for awhile then put them back into the box when it was time for me to go home. Once home, I told my sister of the ducklings, and she was excited to see them, planning a visit for the next day.

Over the next few weeks, we all watched as the ducklings started to grow, turning into full sized ducks. Their soft fluff was quickly replaced with feathers. They had become accustomed to being held, and we picked them up to hold them often.

One afternoon Nick and I were in his yard with the ducks. We thought that it was strange that they never tried to fly away. I chased one of the ducks on the grass for a few steps, then scooped it into my arms with little resistance. As I approached back to Nick, I gave the bird a small toss. Nick caught the duck and tossed it back to me. We were standing a few feet apart, tossing the bird back and forth with positive words of encouragement. Wanting to see if the duck would take flight. Its small wings flapped as it traveled between us. The ducking squawked as it tried to fly. We continued to pass the bird between us, taking a step backwards after each unsuccessful attempt at flight. After a while we had quite the distance between us, and the duck would flap its wings between catches. Two or three big flaps, then sent back the other way. I caught the duck and sent it back towards Nick. It landed in his hands, motionless.

"You killed it, you killed it!" Nick shouted as his eye began to fill with tears.

I rushed over to see the lifeless bird, with my own tears barely contained. Nicks mom, hearing the commotion, came rushing out of the house. She noticed the dead duck in Nicks arms and told me I should go home. I left with my head hung low and my heart filled with sadness.

Later that night, my parents got a call and were told about the dead duck. After that conversation, my parents decided that the right thing to do was to replace the mallard. So, my dad went out to buy the neighbors a new duck. When he returned home, he explained how he had no luck getting the single duck.

"I tried to get a duck," he said, "but the man wouldn't sell me one duck." Dad explained, starting to get fired up "I told him I wanted a duck," "but he wouldn't sell me one duck." Dad took a dramatic pause, and I took the bait.

"Why, wouldn't he sell you the duck," I asked with great concern, anxious to resolve the conflict with my friend.

"Because" dad continued with a smile starting to form on his face, "he would only sell me three ducks!"

Dad took the ducklings over to Nicks house to make good on the replacement. Nick's dad, Joe refused to take more than what was owed, so my dad returned home with the other two ducklings. My sister and I were ecstatic, as we had always wanted a pet, and now we had two.

The Adventures of Donald & Daffy

We were just kids and weren't overly creative when choosing the names for our new pets. My sister and I, after a quick deliberation, settled on the names. Ducks need to have names that start with the letter "D" after all, so with very little arbitration the ducks were named and started to live in our backyard. Donald and Daffy were welcomed into the family and we were excited to have them.

Dad built an encloser to keep the ducks safe in the evenings. The ducks had a large box built. Dad framed out the cube and encased it with chicken wire. This was enough of a barrier to keep them in, and the neighborhood cats out. The rest of the time the ducks had free reign of the yard. We had a small plastic pool that was filled up with a few inches of water for them to paddle in. The backyard was a cozy duck sanctuary.

We watched as Donald and Daffy went from the fluffy little creatures to feathered and robust little ducks in just a matter of weeks. A duck grows to ninety percent of its full size in just seven weeks. I would splash into the pool wearing my cowboy boots to catch the ducks. I didn't want to miss a single moment of them not in my arms. We were always gentle when we held them, they seemed to enjoy the attention. We promised to never try and teach them to fly. I was still sad about the last unintentional fatality and would never try that again. When my sister and I would play in the yard the neighbors tabby cat would prowl along the fence, waiting to find an unsupervised moment to attack the ducks. I kept a vigilant watch and never left the ducks unattended. When we would go in for dinner the ducks would be herded into their protective box.

One evening after dinner I went out to check on the ducks and the tabby cat was sitting on top of the enclosure. The fat cat was licking his lips and taunting the birds while dreaming of its next meal. I took the broom that was next to the back door and chased the cat away. I took a big arching swing with the broom, missing the cat, and hitting the enclosure. The strike from the brook stick misshaped the chicken wire, caving in the top of the box. The birds still had plenty of room to move around but needed to duck down when they passed the dented side of the box. Dad was not impressed with the damage and threatened a swift kick in the pants if it happened again.

Saturday night we needed to have a family meeting on the future of the ducks. Our neighbors across the street had never intended to have the ducks as pets. They were livestock and were being groomed to be fat and delicious. Once the original birds were fattened up to the desired weight, they were turned into an Italian culinary masterpiece. We needed to decide as a family what the fate of these birds would be. Mom was a great cook, but we weren't interested in eating the newest members of our family.

Dad laid out the facts and gave us two fair options. "We can send Donald and Daffy across the street and have them cooked for dinner." He proposed "Or we can release them into the wild, where they can be free and happy."

My sister and I stared at each other with tears forming in our eyes. We were not happy about either of the options, but freedom sounded better than dinner, so we made our choice.

"Freedom." We both said in unison.

"Good," dad said as the final authority on the matter. "I will take them to the farm when I leave for work on Monday."

Mom nodded in agreement "You can say your goodbyes tomorrow."

Sunday evening, we gave the ducks their final aggressive hugs, and when we woke up Monday morning they were gone from the yard. The enclosure looked gigantic and out of place without the ducks. We were sad for a few days, as the yard was void of the squawks and grunts that the pair of ducks made. We helped mom overturn the pool that was filled with smelly pond scum and duck shit. A title wave of water washed into the lawn, disappearing into the dry ground, leaving behind the fluffy remnants of the ducks. The box enclosure was disassembled the following weekend. The chicken wire was rolled up neatly, to possibly be used on another pet project, or just in moms garden to hold up the peas. After a few days the yard was back to a pre-duck state, and we started to get over their departure.

For years to come every time we were at the park and saw a pair of ducks that looked even remotely like Donald and Daffy, Mom or Dad would point them out. This helped to reinforce that we had made the right decision in setting them loose in the world. It was always nice to see an old friend, even if there way no way to know for sure if it was actually the same pair of ducks.

Second Chance for Trouble

Before the start of the fourth grade, our family moved to a new house across town. I left behind my friends and classmates, but I was going to miss Corra, Rusty and her grandmas oversized chocolate chip cookies the most.

The new neighborhood felt like it was on the farthest edge of the city. The new house we moved into was built specifically for our family. My parents got to choose all the internal details, like the color of the carpet and walls. I wasn't entertained by such details and only cared that my bedroom would be larger than the last one. It was, now I had space for a bookshelf to keep all the story books I got at Christmas. The bookshelf had an entire level for just my nicknacks. Front a center were my totem pole replicas, they were flanked by a large chunk of fools' gold my parents brought back from Nevada. I had some model cars to fill out the rest of the space. I was happy with my new room, my sisters' room was the exact same size, so we had no conflicts over the space. The whole house was bigger than the one we previously inhabited, we were all happy and excited to grow into it.

The neighborhood was built around a previously established golf course that was built over a garbage dump. There were still miles of open space to develop before all the houses would be built and the neighborhood would be considered complete. We had one of the first houses built on the main street, with an empty lot on the right side of our new house and a couple more built in the other direction. My sister and I were excited to watch the homes get built, hoping that the inhabitants would be our ages, and we could make some new friends.

The move also meant that I got to start at a new school at the beginning of the fourth grade. It was a giant school with a multitude of grades crammed into one massive building. Valley View was humongous compared to the smaller school I had just left behind. These kids were all giants, rushing from room to room. I could barely see through the mass of humanity and was quickly lost in the maze of unknown hallways. Once most of the students had gotten to their classes, the hallways were empty enough for me to navigate my way to where I needed to be.

The classroom I spent my days in was just a square box of a room. The desks were setup in rows in the middle of the class. A stained chalk board was at the front of the room next to the teacher's desk. All our bags and shoes were left at the back of the room. I quickly became friends with the kid in the desk next to me. He was from Egypt and was good at drawing the hockey team logos.

I didn't have long to get settled into that school before we got moved to another one. The parents of our new neighborhood were not happy with the original designated school. All the students in the neighborhood would need to be bussed to Vally View and some of the parents wanted the neighborhood kids to be somewhere closer.

"Why are we changing schools again?" I asked my father. "I was just starting to make new friends." I said frustratedly.

"I know it's a pain." He spoke. "You will make lots of friends at the next school."

"But why, we just got there." I persisted with the question.

"The other parents aren't happy with that place." He told me. "The other moms heard something about a kid bringing a knife to school." Dad started to explain. "Probably to cut the steak they brought for lunch," making light of the situation. "Now the community wants to change schools, that's just the way it is." Dad said. "Welcome to the neighborhood."

I nodded in acceptance.

On Monday the yellow school bus arrived and took us to our second new school. Andrew Sibbald elementary was where I would spend the next three years. The school was big and bright. The school was divided with the small grades, one two and three, on the one side of the school, and the other grades four, Five and six on the other side.

My sister was attending the same school, but I never got to see her during class hours. She was small and took her lessons on the other side of the school, with the other grade two students. The kids from the smaller grades had a different field to play in at recess and lunch, so our paths rarely crossed. We only saw each other on the bus ride to and from school.

The grade four class was all the way at the back of the school. You needed to walk the entire length of the hallway to reach the space that was designated for the fourth grade. The hallways were lined with a generic grey tile found in all educational buildings. There were no doors on most of the classrooms, the open concept was strange but inviting. All the classes had the same short grey carpet. The whole school was just a rectangle with the center being the library that both sides of the school could access.

In the library was the computer lab, the doorway of the off-limit room emitting a green glow from the new single-color monitors. I was excited to use the new technology as this was the first time I had even heard about computers.

I sat in the last row of desks at the back of the classroom. I kept my head down and my mouth shut. I managed to go unnoticed for a couple of weeks. Finally, one day I was called on to write something on the chalk board. I walked to the front of the class and picked up the powdery cylinder and scratched my answer onto the board. The squeak of the chalk was unintentional, and the class burst into groans as they all covered their ears. I went back to my seat quickly. The teacher then asked me a follow up question to something that was on the board. I must have squinted at the faint markings for too long because she asked me to change desks.

"I think you will have an easier time up front," she said sweetly "then I can keep an eye on you." She said with a friendly smile.

I moved desk locations without any fuss, not wanting to waste the fresh start on something so trivial. But I was now front and centre to the black board. This forced me to be more active in the class conversation, forcing me to participate. Whenever the teacher saw my attention waiver, she would prod me back in line with a topical question. I didn't mind, it was just a change from being invisible in the back of the room.

After a few weeks of being at the new school all the parents were called in for a meet and greet with the new teachers. I was given a positive review for my participation and eagerness to help around the class. My parents were surprised by my glowing review and were waiting for the big but.

Dad couldn't wait any longer, "but?" he enquired.

The teacher smiled, knowing that my parents expected some sort of negative spin on my behavior.

"But" she started, "have you ever taken Thomas to have his eyes checked?" "He might be having a hard time seeing the chalk board."

She then explained how I was moved from the back of the class, up to the front, and when that happened, she saw drastic improvements with just that simple adjustment.

"I will make an appointment for next week," Mom said.

She was happy that there were some suggestions to try and make my learning easier. My parents got up and thanked the teacher for her time. Dad reached up and adjusted his glasses out of habit, as they left.

The next week I was sitting in the chair at the eye doctor's office. It was a small office with a big chair, my feet didn't come close to touching the floor when I sat in it. Mom and I waited for the specialist to come in and give me the eye exam. The doctor soon arrived in his white coat and asked us some questions. I was then instructed to lean forward in the chair and a large set of oversized binoculars were pressed into my face. They hung on a heavy arm that could be adjusted in multiple directions at once. The nose rest was cold, as it was adjusted into position on my face.

"Can you see the letters on the wall?" the doctor asked with his breath smelling of coffee and cigarettes.

I nodded.

"Don't move, don't nod, just say the letters you can see on the wall, ok." He said firm but friendly tone. "Be honest if it changes, and if the focus doesn't change that's alright." He explained. "There are no right answers, but the more accurate the answers are the better we can figure out what kind of glasses you will need." "Ok, tell me what you see," he asked.

"F, U, Q" I read off the wall.

"Good, now what if I change this?" he asked as he rolled one of the wheels on the mechanism. The letters on the wall changed focus and were easier to see.

"Yes, I can see them better." I said excitedly.

"And now, and now, and now." He continued to move the wheels, and the letters were getting clearer each time.

I made confirmation each time the wheels turned, and the letters got better. The doctor would sometime turn the dial the other direction to see if my answers changed, but I kept telling him how I saw the letters. Good or bad. Once we finished that exam, he pushed the heavy arm back out of the way.

The doctor squared up his chair and sat directly in front of me. He held out a light and asked me to follow it with my eyes. I moved my head as the light passed left to right. He clicked off the light and began to give his diagnosis.

"Thomas is going to need glasses." he started to explain. "He has astigmatism, that means that his eyes are not perfectly round, and that slight curve change causes his vision to blur at a distance." The doctor continued. "I would recommend a bifocal lens." He went on, "that will also help with the near vision and make the letters when reading more focused."

"Also," he continued, "Thomas moved his head when asked to follow this light," he paused. "You might want to check with this specialist to help strengthen the eye muscles."

The doctor handed mom a business card. Mom thanked him for the referral, and we left to find my first pair of stylish glasses.

The glasses store was filled with hundreds of different choices for frames, but they were all really the same. Nerdy.

So, I picked out a basic pair, that I didn't hate, and got the prescription filled. An hour later I was walking out of the store wearing my new glasses. The floor of the mall felt crooked as I looked through the new lenses, the glasses were going to take some time to get used to.

The results back at school were vastly improved. I was able to see the chalk board clearly from my desk, and words in the books were in perfect focus. Wearing the glasses was an immediate improvement to my learning, even if I looked like a nerd, and was the youngest person to ever to wear bifocals. The line on the lenses dividing the glass was barely noticeable. None of the other kids said anything about my new glasses, which was lucky, because kids could be vicious, and I wasn't one to take kindly to being bullied.

Eye School

Mom didn't waste anytime making the appointment for me to go see the eye specialist. Within a week were waiting together in a new office, eager to see what needed to be done to improve my sight. We got called up by the receptionist and directed to a second waiting room. It was a larger room with a table and chairs in the middle. A white board was on the back wall, and a large grey box with lots of buttons was just inside the door on the front wall. We only waited for a moment before the specialist walked in, greeting us with a smile.

"You must be Thomas," she said warmly. "Let's see if we can't get those eyes moving." She pulled up a chair and sat in front of me, pulling out a wooden stick with a red circle painted on the front. "Follow this with your eyes, try not to move your head, and follow along," she instructed moving the stick in front of my face. "Ok, it looks like your eye muscles are weak," she explained, "so we will do some exercises to help you get them strong and healthy."

Mom and I just sat there listening to the instructions, not knowing enough to ask any questions.

"I'm going to have you do this test here," she pointed to the buttoned box on the wall. "Stand on this wooden box and press the buttons when they turn red."

I stood up and got on top of the wooden box that made me a few inches taller and waited in front of the grey box with the buttons for more instructions. There must have been fifty buttons on the panel waiting to light up.

"Ok now look straight ahead and when the red light comes on, reach out and press the button." She explained, reaching up high onto the side of the box to turn it on.

I waited for the first red light, it turned on, I reached out and pressed the button. There was a squeaky electric tone when the button was pressed. Another button turned red, beep, then another, beep. The exercise ran about thirty seconds, and I had pressed ten buttons. I was happy with the results as I had pressed all the lights that I saw turn on.

"Thank you, you can go back to your seat," she instructed. The specialist looked over at my mother and said, "did you notice how many he didn't see?"

I was confused, but mom nodded in agreement.

"Let's make another appointment for next week," the specialist suggested "but over the week you can practice with the stick and dot." "I also have some writing exercises to help strengthen the hand eye coordination."

I wasn't happy about the homework, but we thanked the doctor and made arrangements for the visit next week.

We got back to the car, then I asked mom about the missing red lights.

"I pressed all the buttons, didn't I?" I asked with confusion.

"You, did not," mom said gently, "you really didn't see the other lights?" "There were probably ten that went off that you didn't even react too." She explained.

"I pressed everyone that I saw turn on," I confirmed.

"Well, I guess we got some work to do then," she said with a smile. "Let's go get some lunch, then I will take you back to school."

"Cheeseburgers?" I said with excitement.

"Sure, why not." Mom agreed. "Let's go."

We went to the mall and had lunch in the food court. I had a plain cheeseburger and a root beer, mom had something similar. This would be our new tradition after eye school, cheeseburgers at the mall. It was the best day of the week, even if I did get homework.

After a few visits to the clinic the improvement with my eye motion was visible. I had the full use of my eyes again and could press all the red buttons except for one. The taunting red light was off to the left and was physically out of my reach, but I could see it. Mom was impressed by the change from the first visit to the last. I hated to do the lettering exercises, and it was a battle to have me get the task done. Mom would only let me read from my favorite bigfoot book if I finished all my eye school homework, so I suffered through the tedious task. We continued to work on the eye exercises for the rest of the school year, making sure that I was in the best form to take on the fifth grade.

Shadow People

I was in bed and asleep for hours. I awoke to the rest of the house being quiet, everyone was lost in their dreams. I stepped off the bed onto the carpet and walked slowly towards the kitchen. I was awoken by my nightly habit of needing a glass of juice around the witching hour.

I walked with small steps towards the kitchen, not making a sound as I passed by my parents open bedroom door. I got down the hallway and stepped into the kitchen. The coolness of the kitchen floor felt good, in contrast to the warm thick carpet. I moved towards the fridge and pulled open the door slowly. I retrieved the container of apple juice and closed the door part way. I moved over to the cupboard to grab a small glass from the elevated shelf, using the light from the fridge to see inside. I used both of my hands to set down the glass, trying to not make a sound. I poured the apple juice into the glass, just past half full, then returned the cardboard container to the fridge.

Once the fridge door was closed the kitchen was in medium darkness, my eyes adjusting to the minimal light. I returned to my glass of juice and sipped it down slowly. My eyes adjusting further to the darkness. The cold glass of juice taking the dryness away from my throat. Once the glass was empty, I placed it on the counter next to the sink, carefully with both hands. Once the glass was put down, I started back towards the warmth of my waiting bed.

As I approached the transition between the kitchen and the living room I stopped dead. In the bay window of the living room was a silhouette of someone. The window was elevated to the second floor of the house, so my sleepy mind was confused by its position. I didn't move a muscle, just watching as the figure stood in the illuminated window. Light poured into the room from the streetlight that was in front of the house. I waited for a few moments until the shadow noticed my presence. It turned, looking over its shoulder without moving. There were no facial features visible in the dimly lit room. Disturbed by my presence it fully turned and charged towards me. I stood my ground, frozen in place. I wasn't scared, but I felt the hair on my arms stand up. A chill ran over my body, and I shivered. The shadow zoomed past the edge of the sofa, turning towards the hallway. It quickly turned down the stairs, a dark shadowy trail following behind it. The shadow phased through the front door, disappearing into the night.

I stood in the kitchen doorway, my feet stuck on the cold floor. I took a moment to process what I had just seen and moved forward towards the front room window. I got to window and looked out onto the street. I watched as the shadow crossed over grass that divided the boulevard, its dark trail still following behind. Once it hit the sidewalk on the other side of the road, it zoomed up the hill and out of sight.

I stood in the window for a few more seconds, waiting to see if it came back down the street. Then I quickly moved with haste, and less concern for making noise back towards the warmth of my bed. I got back to bed and pulled the blankets up to my chin, staring up at the ceiling. I replayed the moment back in my mind and decided that the spirit must not have been evil, or I would have felt some sort of primal fear. That thought calmed my mind enough to close my eyes and return to my nightly slumber.

When I awoke the next morning the memory of the ghost was hazy, but I know what I had seen, and my empty juice glass was on the counter, so the whole event must have happened. I didn't tell anyone about the encounter, not wanting to be told I was just being silly. I know what I saw, the memory of my arm hairs raising as the apparition went past locked into my mind.

Camping is Fun

The summer started off great. The house next door was starting to be built, and I giant hole was dug in the ground. My sister and I never missing an opportunity to have some fun and got some boxes from the laundry room. We unfolded the cardboard to make a pair summer sleds out of the apple juice cases. We rode the boxes off the edge of the new hole into the bottom of the newly formed pit. It was a bit rocky, but you could pickup some good speed going down the steep slope. We had a few afternoons to play in the hole before the house foundation was poured. The new concrete barriers made sliding down the hill almost impossible, with the blockades at the bottom.

After a few weeks we were starting to get used to the new neighborhood and started to explore further away from home each day. There wasn't much to find, there were only a couple of streets built, and dirt for miles. So, we were excited when our parents told us that we would be spending a week away from the house camping with our grandparents.

Six Lives Left

Dads' parents picked us up in the motor home and we started our summer adventure. We started out on the road and went to the campgrounds that were just a few hours away. We visited the small towns that were scattered around the prairies, our favorite camp site was in Okotoks. It was a large campground with access to the river. We would splash and play in the shallow water most afternoons. In the evenings we would push our way through the trees and bushes at the back of the campground. Once we got through the brush the world opened onto the baseball field. We would watch the players practice for a few nights, then they would play an official game on the weekend.

My sister and I quickly found out that if we watched from beyond the outfield fence, we could return any of the wayward balls for a fee. We would get a quarter for every ball that was hit out of bounds and returned to the umpire. I was older and faster and always managed to return more of the balls, but we split the rewards evenly every night. The quarters were quickly traded for candy at the campground store. It was a great summer, especially with a small paper bag filled with sour candy in my pocket.

One of the mornings Grandpa and I were going out for an adventure to pick some berries that he saw a few days back. We left early and worked our way through the trees until we got to a barb wire fence. Grandpa held the wires apart as I climbed through. I watched where he put his hands and pulled the wires open for him to pass through without getting caught on the sharp barbs. We wandered down the trail on the other side of the fence until we got to the saskatoon berry bushes.

Thomas Neamtu

We used the pails we brought with us to collect the perfectly ripened berries. In true berry picking fashion I ate more then ended up in the bucket. I had the bucket filled halfway with the juicy berries, my fingers were stained purple and my lips matched. I was ready to go back to the campground, my fingers were sore, and my belly was full. I made my intentions clear that I was finished with the berry picking and told grandpa that I was going back. Then I left. He wanted to stay and get more of the berries and told me to stay. But I was done so I left without him, I knew the way back and didn't give it a second thought.

I made it back to the motorhome with my bucket of berries and was greeted by grandma. She was excited to see all that was picked and had plans to make a saskatoon berry pie. Grandma made delicious pies. I turned in all the berries and went on about my day, wandering off into the campground.

Grandpa showed up a half hour later and he was angry. He was not impressed by my insubordination and me leaving him abandoned in the field. Evidently, he had some trouble getting back through the barb wire and put a hole in his shirt. I managed to get through the wire without any problems and made sure I told him so. This enraged him further and he grabbed hold of my arm and pulled me over his knee. Before I even knew what was going on I was being spanked with his leather slipper.

I started laughing as the leather slapped my back side. The sound of the slaps were louder than the non-existent pain the sandal swats caused. Grandma ran over to see what the commotion was. Seeing my legs flailing as grandpa swung again.

"You're killing him, you're killing him!" grandma shouted to us.

I don't know which one of us she was speaking to exactly, I was laughing hard with a red face. Grandpa was walloping me with the slipper his face also a deep crimson. He laid down one more loud smack before he gave up and dropped the slipper. I went outside quickly, with my cheeks burning, from laughing so hard. His slippers didn't even leave a sting. I waited out there until I was called in for dinner. I re-entered the motorhome and sat at the small table inside. Grandma was opening a can over the table.

"I'm not eating that," I said with disgust.

"What this, its delicious." Grandma said.

"I'm not eating cat food." I said firmly "you can't make me."

Before grandma could say anything, my sister had sided with me.

"Yea, I'm not eating cat food either." Lisa said, looking equally disgusted.

Grandpa chimed in "It's not cat food," he said angrily "it's spam."

"I don't care what it is, I'm not going to eat it." I said firmly.

"You kids are spoiled." Grandpa griped. "Its this or nothing." He said laying out the ultimatum.

"Then its nothing, because I'm not eating cat food." I said, leaving the table.

Grandma looking concerned about our lack of dinner asked "Well, what do you want then?"

I responded, "Apple sauce."

It was a great summer, and truly is one of my favorites. The conflicts I had with grandpa are some of my fondest memories.

We finished out that night camping in the motorhome and were promptly returned home the following day. Grandpa told my dad of our refusal to eat the spam. Dad told him that he wouldn't have eaten that cat food either, Grandpa pouted in defeat.

A Career in Forgery

The fifth grade was another great year for me to push the boundaries of my trouble making skills. Every Monday we would have a spelling test. We were expected to study over the weekend and practice the predetermined words. I never did homework, ever. So, I was not always as prepared for the quiz as the other students might have been. I would normally get seven or eight of the words correct and I was alright with that. Any of the words that were misspelled, the teacher expected the students to write them out ten times each, as homework. Everyone knew the task, and the rules of the spelling tests. I don't do homework, and the rules don't apply to me.

The expectation after the tests were marked was that the list of misspelled words would be written out ten times each. Needing to be returned the next day with no further problems. If the punishment exercise was not completed, the words would need to be written twenty times each. The words required for the assignment would grow, adding ten more words for each additional day the assignment was incomplete.

By Friday I had racked up a total of over one hundred and twenty words.

Ms. Moffat found this to be unacceptable and sent a note home for my mom to sign in acknowledgement of my still growing incomplete assignment.

"This needs to come back on Monday, with all your words finished." She warned.

I didn't dare talk back and nodded with understanding. But there was no way I was getting that note signed.

I returned to class on Monday with hopes that the teacher had forgotten about the note and all the words. She had not. I was asked for the autographed page early in the day and informed her of my misfortune.

"My dog ate my homework." I said with a smirk. She did not fall for my clever excuse. How did she know I didn't have a dog.

"Come with me," she said, "we are going to call your mother."

We walked out of the classroom and into the library to use the phone. The other students watched my departure, whispers filled the room, uncertain of my return.

My body was getting warm, and I could feel all the blood rushing to my face. My pulse was thumping in my ears as I quickly planned how I was going to get out of this mess.

Six Lives Left

We got to the small desk in the library and Ms. Moffat picked up the phone and handed it to me.

"Call your mother and tell her about your incomplete homework." She instructed.

I started to dial the phone, intentionally missing one of the numbers. She noticed my tricky fingers and told me to give the number so she could dial. I told her the number "236" (should I tell you the number? mom would love the call.)

Mom answered on the second ring, "hello."

"Hi mom, its me Thomas." I said flatly.

"Hello, what did you do now?" she asked her tone quickly turning annoyed.

"Well, it's what I didn't do," I started to explain "I forgot to have you sign a homework note, for some words I misspelled."

"Oh, is that all?" she said, "is your teacher there?" she asked

"Yes," I responded and handed the phone to Ms. Moffat.

They had a quick conversation that I ignored while staring down at the desk. I knew I was going to be in trouble when I got home, and it was going to be a long day. Ms. Moffat hung up the phone and we went back to the class.

When I got home, I was greeted by mom and she signed the note, but only after I had finished writing out all the words that I owed the teacher. It was a long night, but I finished.

Calling home on Mondays became a regular event. I never did the homework and would always delay getting the note signed until the last possible moment. I spent more time doing the extra work than if I would have just done it right in the first place. But I liked the conflict and needed to fight against the authority, even if it wasn't in my best interest. And getting out of class to call home had almost turned into a joke.

After a few weeks of getting mom to sign the notes I had the great idea that I could just sign her name. Mom's signature is beautifully handwritten and hasn't ever changed. I pulled out the signed note from the week before and lined up the pages. I went the desk in the laundry room and pulled out a writing utensil. I double checked that the signature was visible through the top page. It was faint but I could see it well enough. My nervous hand trembled as I traced over mom's cursive. The finished work looked pretty good, and if the signature wasn't given too much scrutiny, I thought it would pass as hers.

Tuesday morning, I went into class with my head held high, ready to turn in my forged homework note. If this worked out, I had just cracked the fifth grade and would never have to do homework ever again. I stood in front of Ms. Moffat's desk and rummaged through my backpack for the note. She extended her hand, flexing her greedy fingers waiting for the crinkled page. I pulled it out and handed it over.

Her laugh caught me off guard. She was normally very stoic, and I think that was the first time I had ever heard that sound come from her.

"Nice try," she said with a tiny smirk "Mom's don't sign notes with purple pencil crayons."

She shook her head at the shear audacity of me to try and pass off the less than stellar forgery. "Let's go call your mother."

After a month of phone calls home mom was aware of my spelling shortfalls and expected the call on every morning at nine. It was just like clockwork. Mom started to get mad at my constant refusal to do the work on time and after my lame attempt to sign her name, began to ask to see my spelling tests each week. I was forced to practice before the tests, learning the words early. This forced me to do less of the extra words each week and kept the teacher from calling home every day. Now is a good chance to learn from my mistakes. So, if you're going to forge your mothers signature remember, moms don't use purple pencil crayons, try a green one.

Noodle Soup

I had missed getting a homework note signed for the millionth time, and a new form of punishment was designed to change my insubordinate behavior. I was going to be punished by being forced to eat my lunch in the main office. Most days I would eat lunch outside. Having that hour of fun in the sunshine taken away for the rest of the week was going to be my punishment. But I soon found new ways to be entertained.

At noon I was put into a small office, behind the reception station, with just an old wooden office desk and two chairs. One chair was behind the desk and the other was next to the door.

"Stay in here until I come and get you." Ms. Moffatt instructed as she closed the door.

I sat at the desk and unpacked my lunch onto the wooden desktop. Mom always packed the best lunches, I always had more than I could eat. Her sandwiches were legendary. If I was outside, I could have traded half a sandwich for some cookies.

Six Lives Left

I quickly nibbled all my food and packed the garbage back into the plastic batman lunch box. This was my third lunch box of the year. The last couple had structural integrity issues. When they were used as the bases when we played kickball at lunch. This was going to be my last lunch kit for the year, and if it was broken, I would be forced to bring my lunch in a paper bag.

I searched the desk drawers looking for treasures, anything that was abandoned would soon be mine. All the drawers were empty, not even a stray paperclip. There was a rotary phone on the desk, but I didn't have anyone to call. It was only Monday, and this was going to be a long week with nothing in the tiny room to keep me entertained. So, I devised a diabolical plan and waited to be released. After forty-five minutes in solitary confinement, I was sent back into the classroom.

That night at home when mom was making my lunch for Tuesday, I made a special request. Mom had no problem and adjusted the planned lunch accordingly.

Tuesday at lunch I was put into the small office again.

"Stay in here until I come and get you." Ms. Moffatt instructed again, as she closed the door behind her.

"Yes, I will." I said with a nod.

I didn't plan to go anywhere I had some trouble to cause.

I unpacked my lunch and laid it out over the desk. I pulled the straw off my juice box and pulled off the plastic wrapper. I had asked mom for some chicken noodle soup for lunch, and she had filled the thermos right to the top. I was very specific in the type of soup I wanted; it needed to be the one with the skinny noodles. I unscrewed the top of the thermos and waited for the steam to disperse before I began to drink it with the juice box straw. I had found this out about eating soup with a straw by accident the year before. I thought this was the best time to use the knowledge for some harmless lunchtime evil.

I slurped the noodles up the straw, each one whistled and screamed as the went up the clear bendy tube. The noise echoed in my tiny office and vibrated the walls. I was about halfway through the thermos when the door burst open. I let go of the straw and it sank into the soup.

"Your lucky," the agitated teacher said as she surveyed the room of the cause of the noise. "I thought you were in here with a gym whistle." She closed the door, and I could hear her tell someone "It's not him, I don't know where that sound is coming from."

I giggled to myself and retrieved the submerged straw and continued to eat my screaming chicken noodle soup.

That night when I got home, I told mom how wonderful the soup was and asked if I could have it again on Wednesday.

Wednesday at lunch I was put into the small office again, this was getting old, and I was ready for a jail break.

"Stay in here until I come and get you." Ms. Moffatt instructed yet again, as she closed the door behind her. I didn't plan to go anywhere I still had some chaos to cause.

I sat at the desk and quickly noticed that the room was different from how I had left it the day before. The desk drawers were not closed tight, and everything was shifted slightly. The teachers must have searched the office looking for the cause of the noisy disturbance.

I pulled out my lunch and found the thermos as requested. I pulled the top off and let the soup cool down a bit, while I ate my carrot sticks. I retrieved the straw off the juice box and began to enjoy my deliciously loud soup. The noodles screamed as they were devoured, filling my belly with warmth. I could here a commotion behind the closed door as the teachers rushed around to find the source of the sound. They didn't even bother to check inside my tiny office, knowing that they had given it a thorough search the night before. I finished my lunch, and the horrible screeching decibels disappeared from the office. I sat and waited to be released from my lunchtime prison satisfied with the disturbance I created.

I waited for a while before I decided that they had forgotten about me. Well now, if I was missing actual class this wasn't so bad. The phone on the desk caught my attention again and I picked up the receiver. No dial tone. This was not a phone to call out of the school, it was used for communication between the classes. Each classroom had a phone on the wall. The phones would only ring a couple of times each year. Only if the office needed a teacher during class. All the classes had three-digit room numbers, and a predictable system for classroom identification. 101 would be a grade one class. 401 would be the grade four class. So, I started to make some calls. The phone rang after I spun the numeric dial the three required numbers. I let the phone ring until it was answered by a teacher.

"Hello, Mr. Kalvin's room." The teacher answered

"Hello, is your refrigerator running." I said giggling. Hanging up before I burst into laughter.

Then I dialed over to the next classroom. I made it down to the fourth-grade numbers when the teachers started to stir. They knew that the call must be coming from inside the school and started to gather in the hallway. The open concept of the school let the loud bells of the phones be heard throughout the whole building. The teachers were standing around scratching their heads in the hallway bickering as to the source. Each teacher had visibility of the phones in their classes and knew that an in-class student wasn't playing the prank.

The phones quit being answered when I called, so I would just give them three or four rings before hanging up. Then moving down the list to the next number. The phones bells dinging and ringing over here in this class, then over there across the hall. I was giggling in my office as I pictured the teachers running around from phone to phone. I called into one of the grade six phones and it was answered on the first ring.

"Who is this?" demanded Mr. Prunkle. "We are going to find you!" he threatened.

"No, you're not," I said in the deepest voice I could muster mimicking his tone, letting out a giggle.

I knew they were on to me and quickly hung up the phone. I sat up straight at the desk trying to look as innocent as possible, with my hands clasped in front of me resting on the wooden desktop. A few moments later the door burst open, and an angry Mr. Prunkle appeared, finding me looking like a perfect little angel.

"What are you doing in here?" he demanded.

"Is lunch over already?" I asked with a smirk, knowing that I had been forgotten for well over an hour.

"Get to class." He said with a gruff tone, disappointed that he hadn't caught me red handed holding the phone.

I collected my lunch box and stood up from the desk and walk towards the door.

"See you tomorrow?" I said with a glint of mischievous energy in my eyes.

"No!" he said with a bit of fear in his voice, "your week in here is finished, you will be outside at lunch from now on." He said firmly, not wanting the chaos to continue.

"Thank you!" I said triumphantly, walking out of the room with my head held high at my victory, with a big grin on my face.

I walked in front of Mr. Prunkle the whole way back to class with that grin on my face, ear to ear. The other teachers were standing at the doorways looking down the hallway to see who the cause of the trouble was. As I passed each room the teachers expressions changed from looks of frustration, to looks of curiosity, as to why I wasn't in any trouble. No one knew it was me ringing all the phones for certain. I mean they knew it was me, but couldn't prove it, so I didn't have to face any consequences. I was out of detention two days early from my original punishment, and all it took was some phone calls. Wednesday was a good day.

When I got home form school, I thanked mom for a fantastic lunch and gave her a big hug. She was the unknowing accomplice in my jail brake. Thanks Mom.

I was never put in that office again, the teachers knowing that I would cause havoc the moment the door was closed.

I would have rung those phones forever.

Fair Exchange

Winter seemed like it was lasting forever. The snow was already deep and falling again. It was a great day for some sledding. I went down the street to Chris's house. Dragging my blue magic carpet sled with a thin white rope. The light plastic barely leaving a mark in the snow as it trailed behind me. I knocked on his front door and was instructed around to the back yard by his mother.

Chris and I had planned to use the steep hills on the golf course to sled down in the deep snow. I was bundled up to keep warm and had my best gloves on, keeping my hands toasty and dry. Chris exited the house from the side door, and we met next to the trampoline. He grabbed the red plastic sled from under the trampoline and we walked over to the fence. The snow was wet and heavy as we carved our way up to the chain link fence.

Chris and his brother had spent the last few days making a pile of snow next to the fence, this made the climb over easier. We pounced over the chain link onto the frozen golf course, our boots sinking deeply into the fresh snow. We walked along the fence line, as we got in front of the house two doors down, I stopped in front of the yard. Chris' neighbor had the new GT snow racer leaning up against the fence. This was the best sled on the market, I had only ever seen it on tv. I reached over the fence and pulled it over onto our side of the green mesh.

"I'm just going to borrow it." I reassured Chris. "I'll put it back when were done."

I wasn't going to keep it, and it wasn't being used, so we could have some fun with it for awhile. What could it hurt.

Chris nodded in quick agreement, and we continued to the steep slope of the hill. It wasn't a far walk, just across the fairway of the golf course hole that Chris's home backed onto. The snowflakes were falling with huge flakes, and our footprints were quickly erased. We climbed to the top of the hill, the snow crunching under our boots, getting our sleds into position for the decent.

I rode the GT down with excitement. It had a steering wheel that controlled the front ski, giving the sled some maneuverability in the deep snow. The side rails were wide enough for my winter boots not be dragged behind the sled. It even had a foot brake that would jam into the snow and stop the sleds momentum. It was fun, more fun than my crazy carpet anyway. We played out on the snow-covered hill for an hour taking turns using the borrowed sled. Each ride down getting faster as we flattened out a path.

I rode down the slope with speed, not noticing that a new kid was approaching towards the hill. I slid quickly to the bottom of the hill, launching a cloud of snow into the air after pressing the brakes. The sled stopped and I stepped off into the now dirty snow. I started the climb back to the top of the steep hill. I reached the hills plateau, breathing heavy, my breath visible in the cold air, and waited for my next turn.

"That's my sled." Said the kid who arrived while I was riding down the carved path.

"I'm just borrowing it for awhile." I started to explain.

Uninterested in my reasoning Chris's neighbor James punched me, right in the face. The shot landing between my eyes. The strike caught me off guard and I instinctively responded by punching him in the face. He returned another shot between my eyes, then I returned the same. We punched each other five or six times before I took a step back and handed him the sled.

"Take it, I was going to bring it back anyway." I said, surprised that the punches didn't have any effect on either of us.

The winter coldness must have numbed our brains and made us impervious to each others knuckle sandwiches. James took his sled and rode down the hill. Once he was at the bottom he walked back home. The dragging GT sled leaving parallel tracks in the snow as it was taken back to his yard.

We took our last run down the hill; I used my magic carpet, and it wasn't the same as the superior GT. Then returned to Chris's house to have his nanny make us some hot chocolate.

The rest of the winter we used the same hill. It was the one with the best slope and was popular with most of the neighborhood kids. James's sled was never leaned up against the fence again, it was always stored up on the back deck. When we were both out on the hill, we had no further conflict. We had worked the situation out on our own with a few knuckle sandwiches and no hard feelings.

Wet Socks

The snow quickly melted away in the spring, and the summer arrived shortly after. On one of the particularly hot summer days Chris and I were in his yard playing with the new super soaker water guns he had just got. James, the neighbor from two doors down, had some friends in his yard and called us over.

"Hey, do you guys want to have a large-scale water fight?" James asked pointing to the water guns.

"Sure," Chris said with enthusiasm "let me go get my brother."

"Perfect, see you back here in five." James said. "I'm going to go grab some ballons."

Chris and I went back to his house to get Mikey. Chris yelled into the house and got his brothers attention. Mikey appeared outside ready to participate in the multi-house water fight. Mikey was pumping his water gun as he walked down the driveway. The three of us went back over to the yard where

James was waiting, and we organized into teams. Our team inherited one of James's friends. Both sides disbursed and we went back into Chris's yard to fill up the ballons that were just handed out. The teams were an even split of four kids on each side. We all had our water guns filled and went back to start the epic summer water fight.

I got into the yard and started to make my way around the side of the house towards the back yard. I turned the corner, and an over inflated water balloon popped on my chest, I was instantly soaked. It was hot outside, and the cold water felt great. I continued into the back yard, blasting the pressurised water at the kid that had just got me with the water ballon. Water was flying everywhere. The rubber balloons were popping, splashing out onto the freshly cut grass. We were all having a blast, running around and laughing, dripping from the onslaught.

Once all the water was drained from the super soakers, we retreated to Chris's yard to refill our toys. The other team had a hose in the back yard and held their position to refill. We took turns filling our water weapons and formulating an attack strategy. The goal was to get them more wet than they got us. We were already soaked so any plan was already defeated, but it was going to be fun anyway.

We all returned a short time later to reengage in the next round of water shenanigans. Another folly of water sprayed into the yard, another retreat to refill.

This time I noticed a hose on the side of James's house and didn't follow everyone else back to Chris's yard. I unwrapped the first two coils of the hose and turned it on, filling the tank of my water gun quickly using the nozzle. Now, I had to wait for the rest of the team to arrive back to my position. I didn't want to be the first one into the backyard. I would have been outnumbered and possibly drowned.

As I waited, I noticed one of the side windows of the house was open. An evil grin crossed my lips, as I aimed the hose at the glass. The water vibrated as it knocked off all the dirt and grime from the window. I uncoiled four more wraps of the hose and moved towards the window. I took aim at the inside of the glass and gave it a wash too. Some of the water inadvertently splashing into the house. My team was still not visible, so I blasted a couple of shots with the hose water straight into the house.

I giggled maniacally as I arced the water into the bedroom. I could hear the water landing on the carpet with a satisfying splatter. After about twenty seconds of spraying through the open windows screen, I quickly wrapped up the hose and turned off the faucet. Just as I gave the handle the final twist the rest of the team arrived back from their refill, and we stormed into the back yard as a group.

No one knew that I had just washed down the bedroom carpet. We had a couple more chances to fill up our water guns before the game was called in time for dinner. I went back to Chris's yard for the rest of the fill-ups, not wanting to be caught with or even near the side hose.

I'm sure the first person who walked into that room got the rude surprise of some wet socks. The thought of some soggy socks still makes me laugh. That was the one and only time we ever had the neighborhood water fight, and I don't know why.

Island Fortress

The neighbourhood ended at the top of our street. The endless dirt was only interrupted by the edge of the golf course. The small sliver of grass broke up the dirty wasteland. The nothingness continued for miles. Chris and I would explore the open wasteland looking for treasures. One day we wandered further than normal up the hill towards the green oasis in the distance.

The ground was starting to be excavated for future home development. We followed the deep tire tracks of the heavy equipment. The machines were giant that moved and reshaped the earth and the tracks they put into the ground were easy to follow. The tracks led us to a raised island of dirt, on the edge of the golf course, near the eleventh green. The island was a round pillar of dirt that elevated up six feet above the ground. The raised ground was nearly twenty feet across on all sides. We walked the perimeter of the elevated ground. Searching for a rocky path that would get us to the top of the mound. We used the goat path and crawled up to the top of the dirt pile.

The one edge had a hill that sheltered a dugout at its base. We decided that this was going to be the perfect place to build our secret lair. So, we set out to find some building supplies to start the construction of the base.

We found that if we asked for scrap wood at the new home build sites, we were able to get quite a robust supply of offcuts. The workers had no problems with us taking wood from the large garbage dumpsters, so we helped ourselves. The offcuts of boards and planks were all shapes and sizes, and we weren't being picky. We dragged the pieces back to the dirt island. Deciding that there must be a better way to get the wood back to the base we retreated home to find solutions to our transportation needs and other required building supplies.

Chris had requisitioned his baby sisters little red wagon, and it was handy in the transport of the recycled lumber. I raided Dads' workshop. I removed handfuls of nails from his abundant supply. I took the handsaw saw and a hammer and hiked back to our top-secret site.

We spent the next few weeks building a basic structure on top of the island. The roof was a tapestry of plyboards that were braced together with scrap two by fours. The roof was mostly supported by the top of the hill, it slanted down eight feet and was braced at the bottom by the ground. We had a loose piece of wood that could be slid over to cover the opening. The sliding door would work until we found some hinges. It was a cozy little dirt shack. If it rained, we would stay dry. It was a perfect place to hide away from our siblings.

On the other side of the island, we built a fire pit. I had learned how to make fires while camping with my grandparents. It was one of the skills that Grandpa had taught me on our weeklong excursions over the summer. I would take the old news papers and magazines from the house, and we would set them a blaze. The paper burned up quickly and was easy to contain.

We would go out to the island every day. Almost never seeing anyone out in the dirt field. From our elevated position we could see the occasional golfer, but they never paid any attention to us, they were too busy making **space for golf**. Every time we would arrive back at the base, we would check to make sure that no one had been inside our secret hiding place. No one ever was, as far as we could tell. We would recover or stored supplies from the rafters and start our fire. Burning one of the weekly news papers I got from home, they were never missed from my house. We had a good stack secured in the dugout and could have a fire every day for a month. Once we ran out of the news paper pages, only burning one edition at a time, we would return home in time for dinner.

One day on the way back home we passed hundreds of wooden markers with different colored plastic flags attached. The flags were a thin florescent pink or green plastic, a tight knot held them onto the pointed markers. The wooden stakes had sprouted up over the last few days, but we never saw who was putting them up. We kicked over a few as we walked home. We had gotten about halfway through the wasteland when a pickup truck sped over to our location.

"Hey! What are you doing out here?" the man in the truck asked with agitation. "Did you knock over those markers?"

We didn't answer right away, and he got mad.

"You better go put them all back exactly where they were." The man said as his anger grew, "Or I'm going to get out of the truck and kick your ass!"

We nodded in compliance.

Quickly turning around to go back towards the downed pegs. We stood up a few of the markers and the truck drove away. Once we couldn't see the taillights we started our journey home with haste, leaving dozens of the pink flags still littered on the ground.

As the neighborhood developed so did the different type of scraps we could find. Once the yards were starting to be developed and having the sod laid, we began to collect the scraps of grass to cover our slanted roof. When the grass covered the fortress, it was undetectable. Our structure held the extra weight from the strips of sod. The grass began to grow and thrive on top of the wood, looking long and shaggy in only a few weeks. We played out there on the dirt mound for months before the home builders started to encroach on our undetected territory.

Finally, one day the island was gone, it had been leveled to the same grade as the rest of the dirty wasteland. We walked towards the fortress and was surprised by its sudden disappearance. That night I woke up to a horrible "what if" kind of dream. What if we were inside our totally camouflaged secret hideout when the machines arrived to knock it down. We would have been swept away in a pile of dirt and rock, completely undetected.

After the body heat from the possible danger left my body, I shook the idea from my mind and went back to sleep. I'm not one to worry very long on what might have been, but we were still lucky to not have been there when the machines rolled through.

Island Fortress Part Deux

Now that our secret lair had been destroyed it was time to relocate and rebuild. Chris and I were wandering down by the river and found a new suitable location. It was on an actual island this time and was only accessible by crossing over a bever dam. This spot was part of the park and had no danger of being destroyed by an earth moving machine. The island was off the main flow of the river. If you watched your step while crossing the dam your shoes didn't get wet. This new location of the secret base was closer to the homes being developed, so bringing over the scrap wood was quicker. I continued to raid the nails out of the workshop. The plastic pail full of nails was starting to be noticeably less, but I was never questioned about it. Once we had all our building supplies on the island we started to construct our new base of operations. We would ride our bikes down to the river every day and work on the new project until it was completed. Our bikes would hide on the mainland in the tall grass, where they were virtually invisible from the trail.

We built our fortress using the trees as the cornerstones. The mismatched boards quickly turned into walls as they were attached to the thriving wilderness. The under brush on the island was used to hide and conceal our progress, leaving tools and supplies on site overnight when we left. I had dug a hole in the ground and lined it with smaller boards to keep the tools out of the dirt. An extra piece of broken ply board was used as a cover, to keep the tools safely out of sight. We had spent weeks hauling wood across the water, walking gingerly along the beaver dam, and building our new fort. The river pathway had way more people wandering past, and our construction noise did not go unnoticed.

Saturday as we were working on the soon to be finished fort when an angry homeowner shouted at us from the mainland.

"Hey, what are you boys doing over there?" he inquired angrily, pointing a finger in our direction.

"How about you mind your business." I shouted back.

"I see that you're building a fort on the island, and I don't like it." He complained. "I can see it from inside my house and its an eyesore" The man shouted back.

"Yea, so, what are you going to do about it." I barked back. We were safe on our island, so I was just being rude for fun.

"What if I come over there and beat you ass?" the man threatened. He looked around for away to get across the creek.

"I'd like to see you try!" I yelled back, pushing my luck.

The angry, taunted man found the beaver dam and decided he was going to come across and fight some kids. Chris and I had made contingency plans for just such and event. We had to defend our island after all. You never knew when the barbarians would invade. We both dropped our tools and rushed over to the edge of the island, waiting for him to start crossing the beaver dam.

"Oh, you're in trouble now, just you wait till I get my hands on you two!" The man growled as he started across.

"Bring it!" I pushed back

Chris and I had been stacking piles of large rocks on our side of the creek for just such an invasion. Chris and I started to toss the large rocks into the creek water, splashing up waves of swamp sludge. The clear water quickly became stirred up with the onslaught of incoming rocks. The water splashed onto the dam making the dirt on top quickly turn into a slippery mud. Chris and I took turns dropping the rocks, splashing the water on each side of the dam.

The man crossing was unsure of his footing and took small steps as he moved towards us. Barking threats at us the whole way. This gave us plenty of time to continue tossing the large stones, creating more muck on the top of the dam. The center of the dam had a large gap that needed a big step and almost a hop to clear. The angry man missed the hop and was teetering on the edge of the now slippery dam, with his arms extended, trying to regain his balance. We focused the following tossed rocks next to him, splashing water up the side of his pants. He teetered then gravity finally won, and he leaned too far, stepping off the dam into the cold creek water.

This was our chance to escape. The man was super angry now. He was up to his knees in the creek and sinking fast into the soft mud. He was pulling at his leg, trying to get it unstuck from out of the muddy vacuum. His attention was away from us, as we ran past him along the top of the dam. Chris and I knew every step to take and made it across in record time. We pulled our bikes out of the tall grass, throwing up some middle fingers as we rode home laughing. I could hear his angry shouts of vengeance as we rode home.

"I bet the mud just claimed another pair of shoes." I joked

Chris laughed and agreed, having lost a pair to the muck a few weeks back.

We waited until Monday after school before returning to our less than secret island fortress. We positioned our bikes in the tall grass in case we needed to make a quick escape. Looking over the beaver dam before we crossed over the creek, making sure no one was waiting on the other side. The water had returned to being crystal clear, and I could see all the rocks we tossed in. there were some new trenches in the water from where the man had dragged his legs out of the mud. We crossed over the now dry path across the creek.

Chris and I approached to where our structure should have been standing, only to find charred boards and some scraps of the wood we had used. Someone had burnt down our woodland fortress. Burnt-up boards were still tacked to the trees and the ground was covered in ashes and half burnt sticks. We collected our undamaged supplies and the tools that were still hidden near by. The tools were safe in the hidden hole, evidently undiscovered. I was happy they were not taken; Dad would have been mad if the tools were missing. After a final survey for anything of potential use, we vacated the island. It seemed a bit extreme to burn down our fort, but who were we going to complain to? We didn't know who had set the island on fire, but we had our suspicions. I expected it to be the angry man, who got stuck in the mud. Now shoeless, with a pack of matches, setting our fortress on fire. It was impossible to say, it could have just been some pyro kids, setting trees on fire. We didn't know who had destroyed our work, so we had no one to inflict retribution onto, so we just moved on.

That was the last fort we built; it was fun while it lasted. The rest of the summer we spent riding our bikes and reading ninja turtle comic books. It turned out to be a pretty good summer.

No Cracks

We had been in the new house for just over a year. Dad took great care of the yard. He had built mom a large set of flower beds that filled in the corners of the yard. The grass was cut every weekend, even if it wasn't needed. One Saturday dad noticed a crack on the driveway and didn't think much of it. It's a new home and the ground was sure to settle. However, over the next few weeks the crack got deeper and started to spread out over the pavement like a spiderweb. Dad was not happy with this and put in a claim with new home warranty. The next day the representative from new home warranty arrived and made an official inspection of the driveway. They told my dad that a decision would be made quickly, and the problem would be addresses accordingly.

A few weeks later a letter arrived in the mail. The logo on front was recognized and Dad tore into the envelope with haste, anxious to see when they were going to replace the driveway. Dad's eyes skimmed down the letter, his anger growing as he reached the bottom of the page, signed with warm regards.

"What did the letter say?" mom asked, noticing Dad's agitation.

"It says they are not going to replace the driveway because there are no cracks on it." Dad said as a maniacal grin crossed his lips.

Mom knowing the look in his eye said, "don't do anything crazy." She knew her voice of reason would go unheard and didn't even try to dissuade him from his plot.

"let's go boy," he called to me, "we need to go get a few things."

We left the house and went to the hardware store to get the supplies that Dad needed to get his plan in motion. I didn't even ask what the plan was, but I knew it would be ridiculous as Dad always had a flair for the dramatic.

We returned home awhile later after purchasing a cart full of supplies. It was late and I had to go to bed, so I was unable to help Dad with his planned art project. I would have to wait until Saturday morning to see the results of our trip to the store.

I woke up in the morning and Dad was calmly eating his breakfast at the kitchen table. He was dressed nicely in his normal work clothes, looking professional, not wanting to look like a crazy person. His plan was to sit out in the front yard of the house all day. Explaining his art project to anyone who dare stopped to ask questions and boy did they stop and ask questions. I followed Dad out the front door as he went outside to setup his folding chair. I made it down the front steps and stopped dead in my tracks when my eyes adjusted to the abomination on the driveway.

Dad had spent the night painting over every crack in the driveway with bright red spray paint. It looked like a bloodbath; the spider web of cracks covered the whole concrete slab. The red paint accentuating the depth of the imperfections. He had also plastered a banner across the entire length of the garage door. In big red spray pained letters it read "no cracks!?" The paint ran down the banner making it look even more sinister. The driveway looked like a murder had taken place and it got the attention of every car that passed the house.

Most people would make a turn at the bottom of the hill, making a second pass to get a better look. The letter from new home warranty was also taped to the banner. Its small page just visible from the sidewalk. People were curious enough to walk up the red painted driveway to see what it said, cautiously approached to read the official letter. Lots of people stopped to talk to Dad and see what was going on, looking for an explanation for the eyesore.

Dad's plot was clever, and his stunt worked really well. This was a new neighbourhood; weekends were busy with people shopping for new homes. The new home warranty people were by in the early afternoon, the news of the red driveway spread quickly. The representative pleaded with Dad to wash off the paint as the eyesore was hurting the reputation of community. Dad was having none of it, the only way the paint was coming off was with the destruction of the driveway. They pleaded again with Dad, claiming that his stunt was hurting the future sale of the homes in the area. Dad held firm. After a lengthy afternoon negotiation new home warranty conceded victory and agreed to replacing the driveway. The only stipulation was that my father took down the banner from the garage door. He agreed to that condition but left the lettered taped to the door just in case someone curious wandered by and wanted to know more. The home developers were not impressed by the crime scene that was fabricated on the driveway, and the problem was resolved quickly. The demolition crew arrived on Monday and broke apart the already cracked concrete. We had a new driveway poured within two weeks.

Something That Can't Be Fixed

The driveway was not Dads only conflict with the new home warranty establishment. His next battle was over the drainage of the yard. When the foundation of the house was poured there were errors made in the process. This caused the front yard to droop in the middle. It was the beginning of a potential sinkhole.

A small backhoe arrived to dig a giant hole in the front yard so that the repairs could be made. The concrete front steps hung off the edge of the hole teetering into the abyss. The hole took up most of the yard, bordered by the driveway and the city sidewalk. There was a bright orange safety fence placed around the deep pit to keep people from falling in. I'm sure the orange barrier was just there to prevent me from exploring the depths.

The fence was up for over a week, and it was starting to get the negative attention of the neighbors. One Saturday Dad was loading his golf clubs into the trunk of the car, after making sure everything in his golf bag was in order. As he closed the lid with a heavy thud, he heard a woman's voice behind him. He turned around to greet the lady and was met with an onslaught of angry questions.

"When is this eye sore going to be finished?" the lady started in on Dad. "I'm tired of looking at this mess!"

Dad smiled and responded, "what the giant hole in the front yard, I'm never going fill it," he said with deep sarcasm "I like not to be able to use the front door." He pointed to the front steps hanging over the edge. "I think I might put in a pool."

She was not impressed and scoffed "Well you should fix it soon; it's bringing down the neighbourhood esthetic."

Dad responded sharply "Well you should mind your own business." He was starting to get tired of the bickering.

"Well, the fence is ugly and should be removed immediately," she griped, not knowing she had just given my father the opening he was looking for.

"You know what should be removed immediately," Dad asked rhetorically "you and your ugly face, at least my yard can be fixed, your face, not so much."

Dad turned away and walked up the driveway giggling to himself as the lady stood stunned, standing on the sidewalk. Dad had no fucks to give.

Once he was in the house and the door was closed, he let out a hearty laugh. Mom asked what was so funny, and he told her of the complaint. Mom just shook her head and told him that he was rude, but that wasn't anything new.

Eventually the yard was fitted with some proper drainage and the hole was filled in, closing off the pit to the abyss. The newly contoured ground was re-covered with a thick grass, and everything was back to normal. The front steps rested securely on the ground, and we could use the front door again.

Bus Stop Adventures

Every day of elementary school, I got to ride the yellow school bus. The bus stop was located on a driveway at the top of our street. The bus location seemed random, but I think at some point the kids that lived in that house must have taken the bus to school. The bus would drive its way around the block, picking up the other students along the way, from the handful of scattered stops. The driveway where we stood was the last stop on the circular route of maze-like streets. Once we were on the bus, it would get back on the main street and continue the journey towards our school.

The students that were going to junior high would get picked up from the same driveway, boarding a different yellow bus. Their bus would arrive a few minutes before ours, taking them to the school I was expecting to attend the following year.

The older students would tell us smaller elementary school children what we should expect from the transition into junior high. Wesley was one of the older kids and would share tales of mischief and how he caused trouble everyday. His stories made the wait for the bus entertaining, and the thought of going to the larger school intriguing. Wesley was in grade nine. He would be graduated out of the school by the time we got there, so his shared knowledge was greatly appreciated. Every morning as we waited on the driveway Wesley would get us hyped up with his outrageous stories, more exaggerated than from the day before.

Wesley was always animated and energetic in the morning. Wesley was excited when he found that a basketball that was left out, resting on the side of the house. The rubber of the cold ball slapping the pavement, echoing off into the quiet morning air. Wesley would take shots on the basketball hoop that was on the edge of the driveway. The ball would bounce off the backboard with noisy force. He would try and dunk on the lowered hoop, cheering loudly for himself, when the ball scored the two points from an easily sunk shot. Wesley would toss the basketball at the elevated backboard until one of the parents of the house would come outside and ask him to stop. This request was normally just as the bus pulled up to take him away to school.

Wesley would toss the ball onto the front yard as he stepped onto the bus with an uncaring "whatever."

Then he would shimmy his way through the bus to the very back seat, giving us a wave as it drove away. The wave normally only consisted of a single finger.

We were left outside, standing on the driveway with the frustrated parents, who asked us to not play with the basketball hoop. They would remind us of the early time and of the noise that the ball produced. This was when our bus would arrive, and we would depart from the driveway, not paying any attention to the early morning sermon. The residents of the bus stop eventually made sure that there were never any balls left out over night, and this solved the problem, for a while.

Wesley was always on the lookout for new ways to show off to us younger kids. We were stuck as his captive audience for five to ten minutes every day, and he was an entertainer wanting to put on a show.

It was a cooler fall morning and Wesley wanted to try out a new trick. The bus was due to arrive at any moment. He reached into his backpack and pulled out a small bottle and squirted the contents onto his stylishly ripped jeans.

"Wait until you guys see this one!" He said with a big grin. "The bus driver is going to freak out, she may even have a heart attack."

Wesley approached the edge of the driveway, shaking out the nerves that were building in his hands as the bus pulled up. The bus stopped in front of him and the doors opened. Wesley with a quick motion removed the lighter from his pocket and set his pants on fire.

I could see the sudden burst of light reflecting in the window of the folding bus doors. The driver sprung out of the school bus at breakneck speed. She jumped down the steps, onto the pavement, slapping at Wesley's intentional inferno. Wesley smacking at his pants with little concern, questioned what she was doing. Not pleased the driver instructed him onto the bus and she followed him inside. He worked his was to the back and gave us the daily wave, a big grin and a thumbs up. We all waved back, stunned at the fiery display we had just witnessed.

The next day I was excited to get to the bus stop. We all stood around Wesley and asked him how he had done the trick. He produced the same small bottle from his bag and explained.

"This is lighter fluid." He said.

Squirting a stripe onto his pants, then producing his shiny silver zippo lighter. He flipped the top open and the flame sprung to life. He rested the lighters flame at the top of the spilled lighter fluid, and the pants caught fire in a controlled straight line. He waited a few seconds then patted out the flame.

Wesley then went on to explain the science of the fuel.

"If the lighter fluid is present, I won't get burnt." "The fire will only burn the fuel." "Knowing when to smack out the flame is the real trick, timing is everything!"

Wesley grinned and told us to "Stand back" "I have a surprise planned for the driver today."

We watched as he soaked the front of his pants with the lighter fluid. He had the bottle put away moments before the bus pulled up. The doors opened and we all turned to watch him get onto the bus.

The fireball that emanated from his crotch was massive. The woosh of the flame was amplified as we all held our breath. The kids on the bus all rushed to have their noses pressed up against the windows to see what the flash of light was. Wesley was sanding on the pavement with the crotch of his jeans on fire. He was smacking at his pants with vigor, trying to putout the flames before the abundance of fuel burnt off. The driver pounced out of the bus with fear in her eyes, not knowing what to do. She didn't want to lay hands on a student, especially in the no-no square. After ten excessively long seconds, and probably fifty panicked smacks to his own nut sac, Wesley finally got the flames extinguished.

I could see the relief enter his body as he adjusted his pants and straightened out the backpack straps on his shoulders.

The driver started to yell at him "Sit in the front seat, right beside me!" Her voice trembled, "We are going straight to the principal's office when we get to school." Her face turning red, "this fire show is not going to be a common occurrence, twice was already two times too many."

Wesley sat next to the window and gave us a sheepish wave goodbye, wincing as he adjusted in the seat. We all stood in silence until the bus disappeared. The moment the taillights were out of sight, we burst into burnt weenie jokes. Creating exaggerated stories and reminiscing about the massive size of the fire ball. Now that was a fire crotch.

The next day at the bus stop was somber. We all wanted to know what had happened to Wesley, but he wasn't there. We had to wait for over a week until he returned to ride the bus again. Once we had him cornered, we asked our hundred questions, wanting to know all the details.

Wesley looked at the ground as he explained how he was suspended for terrorizing the bus driver. Telling us how he had all his lighter fluid, and the zippo confiscated, never to be returned. He looked up from the ground with a cheeky grin, telling us of how he had scorched his pubes, saying they may never grow back. We all chuckled. Wesley shot us a harsh look of disapproval, looking for sympathy not laughter. Wesley's bus arrived and he boarded with his head down, back looking at the pavement. He took his new seat in the front of the bus and looked straight ahead, defeated. We all waved as the bus departed, but it went unnoticed. The short time we spent at the bus stop everyday was never quite as entertaining again, mostly because none of us were stupid enough to set our pants on fire. That's a tough act to follow.

Stupid Questions

The seventh grade started just like all the others. I started at Nickle Junior High School; it ran from grades seven to nine. This is where I was being forced to spend the next three years of my life.

After the first few months of the new school year, a report card was sent home. The grading scale was based on just numbers and just like in golf the lowest score wins. My scholastic achievement scores hovered in the middle but were weak enough to garner the attention of the principal. An afterschool meeting was setup with the principal and my parents, and I was required to also attend.

I waited outside the school as all the busses pulled away. I was standing in the school yard after hours waiting anxiously for my parents to arrive, so we could enter back into the school together. They showed up on time and we went inside the school to face my impending doom. The office was just inside the main doors, so we didn't have to go very deep into the building. We were directed to the principal's office from the receptionist, who was packing up for the day. I was upfront and my parents trailed behind me. The office door was open and inviting so we went inside, knocking on the door as we entered. Mr. Latouche was sitting behind his desk and stood up as we entered the room. Mr. Latouche looked like Morgan Freeman. His short hair had a single silver stripe that gave him an instant level of power and respect. He stepped away from behind the desk and shook the hands of my parents.

"Please have a seat," he said with a warm smile. "This shouldn't take long."

The chairs were strategically staggered to have me sit directly in front of the desk with the two chairs for my parents stagged behind mine. We took our seats and waited for him to return to his. Mr. Latouche returned to his position behind the desk and slid his chair to the side. Slamming his hands onto the desk. I sat up straight in the chair my eyes big from the sudden thud of the desk.

"Are you stupid!" he said in a loud authoritative tone.

"No, sir." I said in in small meek voice. Still recovering from the loud smack to the desk.

"What? I couldn't hear you, are you stupid?" he asked again without changing from the elevated volume.

"No sir!" I repeated trying to match his volume, my voice cracking under the strain. Thanks puberty.

"Good." He said as he pulled his chair back into position and took a seat. "Then why are your grades so terrible?" his voice returning to a civilized level.

He sat and waited for me to answer, the silence was starting to fill the room, and I was getting hot. I could feel the blood race into my face and my temples began to throb. We stared across the desk at each other in silence. I didn't dare look back at my parents. We sat in the quiet room until I had formulated an answer for my lackluster grades.

"I haven't been trying very hard, sir." I said, looking back across the desk with anger in my eyes from being called stupid. He noticed a crack in my armor and doubled down.

"Well, if that's all it is," he paused "do you want to be dumb then?" he said leaning back in his chair, showing his total control of the room.

"No sir," I said as the wheels began to turn in my head, trying to find a way out of this conversation.

"Then prove to me you're not stupid and raise up those grades." He said leaning forward, letting the chair push him up to the desk, bring us closer. "I expect to you to do better immediately, and I will be watching." He demanded, extending his hand for a deal maker handshake.

"Yes, sir." I said, having to stand up to reach his outstretched hand.

Our hands met with a solid grip, and we locked eyes.

"Good, I don't want to see you in my office for poor grades again, understand." He said with authority, his grip squeezing my hand tightly.

"Yes sir." I said in agreement, trying to match his firm grip.

"Thank you, now go wait out there while I have a word with your parents." He nodded towards the door and let go of my hand.

I walked out of the office and found a seat in the main office. My hand throbbed as the blood flowed back into my fingers. I waited for my parents and contemplated my options. My fight against authority was at odds with itself. If I didn't do as I was told, I was just proving that I was stupid, and that was not going to happen. Mr. Latouche had painted me into a corner, and I chuckled to myself once I figured out that I was bested. It didn't happen often, but he managed to push my buttons and get the results he wanted. I waited for my parents to come out of the office, and we went back out to the car.

"You know your grounded for the weekend, right?" Dad said more as a statement than a question.

I tried to yell my objection, and my voice cracked again leaving my argument defeated instantly. We drove home in silence. I was not happy about being grounded for the weekend. I was going to miss watching Bram Stoker's Dracula at the weekly sleepover.

On Monday I returned to school and started on my quest to get better grades. The results were immediately evident as I started to put more effort into the assignments. I didn't turn into an "A" student, let's not go crazy, but I did make vast improvements. When I would pass Mr. Latouche in the halls, he would give me a subtle nod, and we both knew that our agreement was still standing strong.

That was the last time I ever had any problems with finishing assignments. I might have waited until the last possible moment to finish them, but they got done as required.

Mr. Latouche had given me the forced motivation I needed to change, and I took the opportunity and never looked back. Thank you, Mr. Latouche, for the well-deserved kick in the pants.

The Wrong Door

I was in front of my locker spinning the lock to put away some unrequired books for next period. I had the easiest lock combination ever, triple tens. Left, right, left, I spun the dial. Garrett was next to me, and we were having a conversation about nothing important enough to change the world. I could hear the slap of shoes coming down the hallway at a rapid pace, the smacks of the treads echoing in my locker. I looked around the edge of my locker door to see who it was. It was Jeff, one of our other friends running down the hall. He ran, passing us by, turning the corner to go down the main hallway.

I closed the locker and turned back to Garrett to continue our mindless banter. That's when I saw that Jeff wasn't running for fun, he was being chased down the hall. Twenty feet behind Jeff was Down Syndrome Pete giving quick chase. Pete was shaking a fist and barking threats as he ran. Pete stopped in front of Garrett and I, gasped for breath.

"Where," he paused, "did he go?" Pete demanded between breaths.

Pete knew we were friends with Jeff, and that he had just went past us. Pete didn't see him take the corner into the main hall and stopped for some directions. Without saying I word I just pointed to the door across the hall. Pete grunted, turned around a busted through the closed door.

Garrett and I looked at each other for a long second, then bust into the most obnoxious laugher ever. Our roar of hysterics caught the attention of a passing teacher, and she looked concerned.

"What are you two up to? She inquired "what could possibly be so funny?"

That's when the screaming started.

Our laughter faded to giggles as we waited out in the hall to see what was going to happen next. The teacher stood next to us and turned her attention to the door across the hall, wondering what all the noise was for.

The first girl bust out of the locker room, holding her clothes against her chest. She was quickly followed by five or six more. The girls were all screeching and yelling as they exited into the hallway. The seventh person out the door was Pete. He had a grin from ear to ear and rushed out of the girl's locker room flabbergasted and confused. He had just had the best day of his life. Pete turned and ran down the main hall as the girls scattered from his path still screeching

Garrett and I started to laugh again.

The teacher solved this caper quickly and pulled us towards the principal's office with a tight grip around our arms.

"I don't know what you did exactly," she said as we were marched towards the office, "but I know you had something to do with all that." "Whatever that was!"

The teacher left us in the custody of the receptionist. We were told to have a seat off to the side of the office. We sat there for a while, occasionally letting out a giggle as we reminisced of the chaos that had just occurred. We waited a long time. Garrett was starting to get nervous; he was normally not in the office and didn't want to get into any real trouble. I told him not to worry about it, I had been here before, and that trouble was a friend of mine.

The door to the vice principal's office opened and we were called inside. We had just hit the jackpot. We took our seats in front of the wooden desk and waited for our fate to be decided.

"So, I don't know what you did exactly." She started "but I know you had something to do with the incident in the girls locker room." She waited to see how we would respond.

I had been here before and saying nothing is the best thing you can do in this type of situation. She waited for a few more seconds to make the silence uncomfortable.

"I hope you had time to think about what you did while you waited." "Those girls were really upset, and poor Pete." She said trying to play on our sympathy.

We said nothing.

The teacher hadn't seen us direct Pete into the change room, all we were guilty of was laughing in the hallway.

"Well, in any case," she said in defeat "don't let it happen again." Getting ready to send us out of her office and back to class.

"I don't think it could happen again," I said unable to resist, "I don't think Pete would fall for it twice." I said with a smile.

Garrett tossed in his two cents "oh, for Pete's sake" he quipped in his best grandma voice.

A flash of anger flickered across her eyes. "You two get out of here, now." Her voice trembling with anger as she pointed to the door. "Before I have to call your parents."

We stood up from our chairs and got out of the office as quickly as possible. Once we were back in the main hallway we started to laugh again. We managed to get back to class before the end of the day. We told the others of how Pete burst into the locker room, caused all the chaos and of our office adventure. I don't think I have ever laughed so hard.

Corner Store Contest

I watched in awe as the homes popped out of the ground all around us. The streets stated to form, and more families started to move into the new houses. One of the most exciting days was when the corner store and gas station opened. Mom had given us some money to go check it out. My sister and I rushed down to the store with our two-dollar bills, ready to get a handful of candy treats. The store was just down the street, and we were old enough to go on the adventure unsupervised.

There was a big opening day celebration in the parking lot. The store owners were handing out free hotdogs and soda pop drinks. We had just hit the jackpot. Lisa and I stood in line to get the free lunch. We ate our delicious hotdogs, standing off to the side of the crowded parking lot. We had just finished the food when the store owner approached. Fred was carrying two packages of something plastic and colorful.

"Doesn't look like you two got your bike accessories." He said with a jolly grin.

He handed us the packages; they were plastic balls that fit over bike spokes. The spheres would rotate with the bike tires making a jingle as the dropped onto the rims each rotation.

"Don't forget to come down for the neighborhood bike parade on Saturday." Fred said, with a big smile. "There will be prizes for the most decorated bikes." He explained.

"Thank you," we said in unison as he rushed off to hand out more of the trinkets. "See you on Saturday."

Lisa and I then went into the new store to find our sugary treats. The store smelled of fresh bread, the warm smell instantly bringing a smile to my face. We quickly wandered up and down all the isles taking a mental inventory of all the future treat locations. The candy that we were looking for was up next to the front counter. The lidded containers were filled with five cent candies, just like the ones we got when we were camping. This was going to be our new favorite spot for sure.

I scanned across the front counter looking for the sour treat I was craving and that's when I saw it. The rack of comic books caught my full attention. I took a few steps over and spun the rack, looking for a book title that looked interesting. I found a brightly colored book and pulled it from the rack. I was willing to give up some candy for a comic book no problem. Especially ninja turtle adventures number two. I went back over to my sister and found she had made her selection. We put all the treats on the counter and paid. We walked home nibbling our candy treats talking about how we were going to win the bike contest on Saturday.

We got home and showed mom our haul of goodies and told her about the bike contest Saturday. Lisa and I then went into the garage to start decorating our bikes. The spoke decorations pressed onto the tires with a bit of force, my fingers were strong enough, so I helped my sister with hers. The plastic balls made a melodic rhythm as the bike moved, taking away all forms of stealth. We had some handlebar streamers. I attached a baseball card into the spokes to make the bike audibly obnoxious. We were happy with the work and waited for Saturday to take our bikes down to the store to show off our designs.

Lisa and I rode our bikes down to the store on Saturday, our parents walking behind us, interested in the neighborhood festivities. The parking lot was full of people taking part in the day. It was great to see everyone all in one place. There were probably thirty kids with there bikes decorated. Our streamers didn't make our bikes the best of the bunch but put us in the middle of the pack. Some of the kids had gone all out on their decorations. They attached cardboard to the bike frames making the whole structure look like something other than a bike. The clear winner had made his bike look like a rocket ship. The top prize was a twenty-dollar gift certificate for the store. The rest of the prizes diminished from there. I was not disappointed in not winning the contest, we still got free hotdogs and a goodie bag.

At the end of the event, they store owner announced that there was going to be a pumpkin carving contest for Halloween. The contest would be held over at the golf course inside the cart garage. He announced that pumpkins would be delivered to every house and that we could expect delivery a week before the contest. Now this was something that I could win, for sure.

After everyone had finished the hotdogs, all the kids got on their bikes, and we rode around the blocks that set the perimeter of the store. Thirty of us rode around in the bike parade down the street, the parents cheered as we all went past. Kids that didn't attend the event at the store, stood in their yards and waived, excited to participate in the event next year. Some children rushed to get on their bikes and took chase, joined in on the caravan as we circled back around to the stores parking lot. It was a great day. After the parade we went home to plan out our winning pumpkins.

Pumpkin of Nightmares

The pumpkins arrived as promised and we got to work on the project Friday night after dinner. Every house had two pumpkins delivered to their front door with a flyer telling of the contest. My sister and I had the whole week to plan out our designs and were excited to get started. We broke into two family teams, boys versus girls, and began to work on the pumpkin projects.

Dad cut off the top of the pumpkin and I scooped out the slimy innards. This was my favorite part of the process, letting the cold slime drip between my fingers as I removed the goop. Dad and I had our idea and went to work quickly. Mom and my sister worked on their pumpkin. We were having our own family contest to see whose pumpkin was going to be judged superior.

Dad carved out an ugly grin into the pumpkin giving it a menacing face. Mom carved out more of a classic smile, making the pumpkin look warm and inviting. After the pumpkins were all carved out and looking good, we cleaned up the kitchen table of all the pumpkin bits and took a rest. Dad looking at the pumpkins resting on the countertop, scratching at his chin, thinking of ways to upgrade our pumpkin. We finished our hot chocolate, and Dad popped a finger into the air, emphasizing his eureka moment.

"Grab the pumpkin, boy, and meet me in the workshop!" Dad said with a new sense of excitement.

I quickly sprung from my chair and pulled the pumpkin off the kitchen counter, following Dad to the workshop.

I was excited to see what enhancements Dad dreamed up. It was late so mom was helping my sister get ready for bed. They would have to wait until morning to see the monstrosity we were about to create. We banged around in the workshop for an hour, laughing as we worked on the pumpkin. Telling each other stories of how the other contestants wouldn't stand a chance against our grotesque Halloween entry. Once we were satisfied with the final product I went up to bed, too excited to sleep. I was anxious for the Saturday contest and dreamed of winning.

Saturday, we got ready to take the pumpkins down to the golf course for the contest, but before we left the house dad wanted to give a big reveal. Dad had covered our pumpkin with a torn-up beach towel to give the big reveal even more showmanship. We waited for my mom and sister to get into the workshop, then he pulled off the towel with a swift motion.

"Tada!" Dad said loudly

"Eww, that's gross" my sister said with a wrinkled-up nose.

"You might have a chance with that," mom said giving encouragement as she looked over at the ugly pumpkin.

"With reactions like that," Dad said, "we might have a winner."

My father pulled the pumpkin from the work bench and took it out to the car, not wanting to damage it before the contest. We all buckled into the car and drove the two blocks to the golf course. The sun was already down, and the fall air was cold. Dad parked the car, and we took our pumpkins out to be judged.

The golf course had moved out all the carts from the parking garage to setup half a dozen tables for all the contestants to display their master works. There were thirty pumpkins already setup on the tables, we found a spot for our pumpkins and put them among the others. Each pumpkin had a number next to it, folded onto cardboard plaque. We thought for a family strategy that we would have our entries on different tables, so that our numbers would be distant. Once our pumpkins were settled in position we went to the first table and inspected the other people's creations. We wandered through all the pumpkins just as the contest was about to be judged.

There were a few categories that the judges were going to base the contest on. One of the judges quickly went over the criteria. Then the three judges took their clipboards and walked down the line of pumpkins, marking on the pages as the went along. Once all the pumpkins were inspected, the judges went off to the side of the room to deliberate and compare their markings. After a few moments the store owner, Fred, stood front and center and the room went quiet, ready to hear the results.

"Good evening, thank you for coming out tonight." Fred started. "We have some great looking pumpkins here tonight, so a big thank you, to everyone and for all your hard work and fantastic imaginations." He continued.

I was starting to get nervous and wanted to hear the results.

"Let's start with the best carved pumpkin." Fred said looking down at his page. "Number seventeen!" he said, as the room cheered.

The crowed clapped as we waited for the carver to approach the front of the room and claim their prize. The boy walked up was thanked again for his hard work, handed a prize, then disappeared back into the crowd.

"Next up let's go with the silliest pumpkin." Fred said with even more cheer from the crowd. "Number six, come on down, you're the next big winner."

We all clapped again as a small girl was gently pushed forward by her father to go claim the prize. Her eyes never left the ground as we clapped and cheered for her lopsided pumpkin with the wonky eyes and the pipe cleaner hair.

"Now let's go with the ugliest pumpkin." He said in a spooky tone.

My heart jumped as I thought this was going to be my chance to find pumpkin carving glory.

"Number twenty-three" he said.

My arm shot up, "that's me!" I said as I moved towards the front of the room. I got to the front and was met with a handshake of congratulations. I'm sure the room cheered like they did for the other contestants, but I was only focused on Fred.

"That is one ugly pumpkin, what do you call it?" the store owner asked, looking for more details on the nightmare.

"That's pumpkin Freddy, from Elm Street." I said with a big grin.

The pumpkin Dad and I made started out as a vicious maniacal grin carved into our pumpkin. Then when we were down in the workshop, we covered the pumpkins orange skin in glue from the hot glue gun. The glue dripping down and looking gross and stringy. We then painted the pumpkin green, giving it that extra level of off-putting fright. The final product made it look as if the pumpkin face had melted off, looking like something truly from Elm Street.

"Well, I'm defiantly not going to sleep tonight," Fred said to the laugh of the crowd. "Good job." He reached out and handed me my prize as I thanked him again.

I was handed a hockey stick; it was white with red painted details, the most significant was a Wayne Gretsky signature on the shaft. I was thrilled and rushed back to my dad to show him my new treasure. He was smiling as I went over retaking my position by his side ready to see the next winner be announced.

The store owner continued to call out numbers like at bingo until every pumpkin number was called. There were no losers that night, everyone went home with something. I felt like I was the big winner with my hockey stick being one of the largest of the prizes. My sister was given some unmemorable prize that was quickly forgotten. But that hockey stick quickly found a home in the back of my closet for safe keeping. All these years later and that stick is still in the same condition as when I first got it. The decorated hockey stick leaned against the wall of the closet for decades, until it found a new home, deep inside my crawlspace for eternal safekeeping.

A Visit from the Grinch

Mom had spent the whole week decorating the house for Christmas. The tree was setup and fully decorated in the front window of the upstairs living room. Hundreds of lights reflected off the gold and silver bobbles that were spaced out to perfection. Mom took great care in the decorating of the annual Christmas tree. The process would take her days, every single decoration had its perfect place, and she took her time.

The weekend before we went out as a family to pick out the best tree we could find. We found one that was not too big and brought it home. It took all week, but the branches had finally settled into position, the sweet smell of pine filled every corner of the house. Mom rushing to get the final decoration set in place before my dad arrived back home from another week of visiting customers on the road. She was excited to see his reaction to the festive remodel of the house.

It was Friday afternoon, and dad was due back any moment. He would come home, change into his weekend clothes, then we would all leave the house for a family dinner at our favorite restaurant. After dinner we would go to the grocery store to stock up on food required for the upcoming week. We did this as a family every Friday; Christmas season was no different. Dad car pulled onto the freshly shoveled driveway, crushing down the remaining stripes of missed snow. I had spent the last half hour pushing off the snow that had fallen after lunch. Dad entered the house, dropping his suitcase at the door that enters from the garage. The smell of pine was fresh, moving into his nostrils, he made mention of how wonderful the house looked decorated. Mom was happy he was home; it had been a long week, she smiled big at the complement to the décor.

In the kitchen we had a quick family discussion on what to have for dinner and settled on pizza. We frequented a place called pizza king III; it was always a safe bet for a delicious Hawaiian pizza. (Yes, I have chosen a side on that debate, and I stand by it! Pineapple forever) We bundled up in our wither coats and loaded into the car, ready for a nice family dinner. As planned every week, we went and got the groceries after dinner returning home a few hours later.

Dad parked the car in the garage. I got out and he popped the trunk, I started to unload the plastic grocery bags into the house. I pulled from the trunk as many grocery bags as I could carry, then took them into the house. I kicked my shoes off on the entry rug and pushed them off to the side, so they would not trip the others as they entered. I used my elbow to lift the light switch as I started up the stairs. I got to the front landing and stopped, my heart sinking, I noticed the front door was opened slightly. I could feel a cold draft as I stood on the top stair. I took another step forward and found a chunk of wood on the floor, just off the floor matt. It felt like I was just kicked in the stomach. A strange feeling washed over me, I didn't know what it was, but I didn't like it. I felt violated, something was wrong, but I still hadn't figured it out. I stood on front the landing, not moving, not knowing what to do.

Mom was next up the stairs and asked what was wrong, trying to push me along. She got behind me and noticed the wood on the floor and she knew what had happened. She nudged me up the stairs to the kitchen for me to put down the grocery bags. Mom dropped her own bags on the counter, then told me to follow her, we went back down to the basement to tell my father that someone had booted in the front door.

Dad unsurprisingly wasn't happy; he grabbed a hockey stick from the shovel rack and told us to stay in the garage. He was going to check the house to make sure that whoever was there, wasn't there anymore. Dad walked into the house, holding the hockey stick high, ready to strike out if the needed. He turned on the lights as he went, checking behind doors and barking threats of violence as he entered every room. He had managed to clear the basement laundry room before I was behind him holding my plastic baseball bat. He looked over his shoulder at me, giving a wink.

"Let's go, chief." He said trying to make light of the situation.

We went upstairs and I turned on the lights for the hallway. There were boot prints pressed into the freshly vacuumed carpet, leading up and down the hallway. The two-tone pattern of moms' compulsive vacuum strokes marked out the path the robbers had taken. I followed Dad closely as we checked the bedrooms and closets. I peeked under the beds just to make sure. I couldn't fit under there, but hey it's better to be sure. Once the upstairs was deemed safe, Dad called for my mother and sister to join us in the kitchen. He told us to stay in the kitchen and not to touch anything. Mom picked up the phone and called the police. Dad did another lap around the house just to make sure everyone was gone.

From the kitchen table I could see into the living room, it was a mess. The Christmas gifts were unwrapped and tossed around the room. There were some dresser drawers on the sofa, their contents spilled out onto the coffee table. Mom left my sister and I in the kitchen, she went to go see what was missing from her room. Her jewelry box was empty, the fancy box was left empty on my parents' bed.

The spike of adrenaline I had received when I noticed the opened front door was starting to wear off and my hands were starting to shake. Mom made some hot chocolate and we all waited in the kitchen for the police to arrive.

I had just finished my mug of hot chocolate when the officer arrived at the door. Dad welcomed him into the house and directed him up to the kitchen. We sat at the table and gave him our statements, no one was home at the time of the burglary so there wasn't much to tell. The officer asked to look around the house to see if he could find any clues. I watched from the kitchen as he dusted for fingerprints in the living room. After a bit he returned to the kitchen table and gave us his professional opinion on how this crime was going to be solved.

"Well, I would say that it wasn't kids that broke in," he started.

"This looks professional, if it was kids," he paused "they would have broken or destroyed everything in sight."

"This looks tidy and planned out." He continued, "see how they brought the dresser drawers into the living room, using the light from the street to see what was inside, not turning on any unnecessary lights."

"That makes me think they have done this before."

"It looks like they only opened the small Christmas gifts, anything wrapped that could be a ring or a necklace."

"I took some prints off the gift tape, but that might be hard to process, especially if you have gifts from relatives."

"I would like to take fingerprints from the kids, on the chance that they touched anything by accident, their prints won't be in the system so they will be easy to eliminate."

I took this moment to chime in "yes, our prints will be in your system."

The officer looked surprised at my candor. "Why, do you think that?" he asked fishing for an answer to my admission of being fingerprinted.

I went on to explain we were fingerprinted as small children just in case we ended up on a milk carton. Mom was always worried and took precautions for the worst-case scenario.

The officer nodded, agreeing with moms over concerned position. He then asked us to go check over the house and tell him what was missing or moved so he could include it in his report. Mom had already known about her jewelry and started with that, as my sister and I investigated our rooms.

I ran down the hall to my bedroom to check on my own treasures. I pulled open the bifold door to my closet and my heart sank again. The box that I kept all my precious marvel cards was missing. I had a great collection of holographic spiderman cards that I had been collecting for the last few years, and the box was gone.

I returned to the kitchen and told the officer of my missing collection. He added it to the report. After a quick listing of the missing items the officer gave dad a copy of the report and told him to call the insurance company to file a claim. The officer wasn't very reassuring in the capture of the culprits but told us we should be somewhat grateful that the house was left in such a tidy condition. The officer complimented my mother on keeping such a clean house and said that the freshly vacuumed carpet gave him some solid clues with regards to the boot prints from the hallway. Dad thanked him for his time and showed him out the front door. Dad closed the door behind him and turned the dead bolt out of habit. The lock mechanism could be seen clearly, not able to hold the door closed with the chunk of wood missing.

I didn't sleep well that night, still with the knot in my stomach, on high alert just in case the robbers returned. They never did.

The next day Dad called the insurance company and made a claim. Within a week the adjuster was sitting at our kitchen table asking questions about the items that were taken from the house. The adjuster went down his list and stopped on my card collection.

"So, it looks like you lost some fancy cards." He asked with a smirk.

Dad rolled his eyes, annoyed at my constant complaint over the loss of the marvel card collection.

"Yes, they took my cards, and I want them back." I said passionately.

"Well, do you know what they were worth, do you have any way to show me the value?" the agent asked expecting me to not be organized enough to know what my stuff was worth.

"I'll be right back," I said holding up my index finger. I ran off down the hallway to my bedroom to get my price guide. I was always organized, even as a kid, I knew what I had and what it was worth in dollars, not just sentimental value. I rushed back holding the price guide and laid it gently on the kitchen table.

"I highlighted the cards that I had, so I could keep track of the ones I still wanted to get." I explained to the insurance man.

He opened the magazine and found scores of highlighted items. The bright green markings showing a great collection.

"You had all of these cards?" he asked surprised by all the markings.

"Yes, sir." I replied with a puffed-out chest excited to see his renewed interest in my cards.

He pulled out his calculator and made a quick tally. "Looks like around six hundred dollars worth of cards, I will add those to the claim."

Dad's jaw was on the table, he had no idea that those silly spiderman cards were worth anything, let alone six hundred bucks. The card collection was the last line on the claim report, so the insurance man thanked us for our time packed up his bag and left.

A few weeks later I got a cheque in the mail for the claimed value of the missing cards. Dad took me around to the comic shops and I recollected the cards that I had lost. Making sure to tell the shop owners that if anyone tried to sell the exact cards we were looking for, they were probably my missing cards. Dad still didn't understand how a shiny piece of carboard could be worth so much money.

I found most of the cards I had lost and was also able to pick out some of the cards that I had always wanted. Over the next twenty years I have finished collecting the desired sets, keeping them safe even today.

Pig Wrangler

After years of the bike parades being held in the parking lot of the corner store, the owners wanted to hold a different type of event as the community had outgrown the location. The store was busy, and a disruption to the parking lot was bad for business. So, the event was moved down by the river. It was re- branded as the mini-stampede and bike parade. All the neighbourhood kids would still decorate their bikes and ride them down to the river for the contest and free hotdog lunch. The river was a great place for the gathering, the space was wide open, and everyone had easy access to the area. There was a perfect clearing next to the water for the barbeques and events to be setup.

I went down to the river with my mom and sister not knowing what to expect. We found that the designated space was decorated with hay bails and a fenced in petting zoo. The event had grown larger over the years and had over a hundred people standing in the field next to the river. A barbeque was cooking the hotdogs fast as possible but hardly keeping up with the demand. All the kids were hungry, waiting patiently in line for there singed hotdogs.

My sister and I had outgrown the bike parade and didn't enter it this year. We watched from the sidelines as the smaller children clapped and cheered for their prizes. Their excitement was contagious, and we were ready to see what events were planned for us, the bigger children.

I recognized some of the kids from school and went over to hang out with them, leaving my sister with her friends. It was Nick and his cousin Wes. Nick was in my class, and I knew Wes from the bus stop. After a bit the store owner, Fred waived everyone over for some instructions. He explained how were going to play some games, keeping score, and the teams with the best record after the events would win the grand prize.

Nick and I teamed up, and his cousin found someone else to partner with. The first game was an egg toss. We took our positions, standing in two rows facing each other. There must have been twenty teams all lined up ready to play the first game. The goal was to see which team could pass the egg back and forth the most times without breaking it.

Fred stood at the head of the line and shouted "go!" raising his arms in the air.

The eggs were tossed into the air, from one side to the other.

Fred was keeping count "one." The eggs tossed back the other way "two." Another toss "three."

The first egg hit the ground making a cracking splat as the shell broke into the grass. Fred continued to count, the eggs falling to the ground the higher the numbers grew. Wes had given up around ten and chucked the egg at his partner, the egg breaking in the kid's hands and splashing onto his favorite shirt.

Nick saw the mischievous glint in my eye and knew that I was going to send the next toss with some extra force. He was still holding the egg, and beat me to the punch, throwing the egg at me hard. I was quick with a sidestep and the egg landed behind me on the ground and broke.

"Hey," I said with a smile.

Nick just shrugged with a grin, knowing I would have done the same to him. I was happy neither of us were covered with the egg. The tosses continued down the line and had made it to a count of over twenty before the last egg was dropped.

The points were recorded for all the teams and went off to the next event. It was an egg race. The objective was where you needed to balance an egg on a spoon. With the egg balanced on the spoon travel a hundred feet, transfer the egg to the other person's spoon. Then have them return to the starting line without dropping the egg. The task seemed easy enough.

We were broken up into five groups of two, only the top three teams from each group would move on. It was a mini egg transfer tournament. If the egg broke you were eliminated from the next race. Nick started with the egg, walking with steady hands down the grass path. We made the transfer, and

I started back the other direction. I was about two thirds of the way back before the egg fell off the spoon. The egg hit the ground but didn't break, so I picked it up and put it back on the spoon, finishing the race with an intact egg. Nick and I finished third after taking a small penalty for me dropping egg.

Wes was in the other heat of racers and was bumping the other players, making their eggs fall off the spoons. Wes had good balance and finished his race in second place. By the end of the first round there were only ten teams left, so we needed to win two more races to be the egg carry champions.

This time I started with egg, walking quickly down the track to trade it off with Nick, who was waiting at the far end. The transfer was smooth, and Nick made it back to the start line in first place.

Wes managed to finish his race also and now we were going to have to face him in the final. I started with the egg again and looked down the field, planning my steps. I could see Nick and Wes trying to step on each others' shoes at the far end, this was going to be a battle. The race started, and I took off with quick strides, pulling away from the rest of the competitors. I passed the egg to Nick with on problems.

I turned back around to watch the rest of the race, just in time to see Wes smack the spoon out of Nicks hand as he passed by. Our egg fell and broke on the ground. Wes looked back to laugh at his cousin, the egg he was carrying rolling off the spoon to the ground. It landed and bounced on the grass, unbroken. Wes looked back towards the finish line; he hadn't noticed that the egg was off his spoon. Wes stepped on the fallen egg as he raced towards the end. The egg squishing yolk onto his shoe.

The other three teams all finished with their eggs intact, so we had lost out on the points.

Fred the store owner rallied for our attention. And gave instructions for the final event. There was still a chance to win the big prize of the day. The last event was every man for themselves. Ten points were up for grabs for anyone who was able to complete the task. Our attention was directed over to the petting zoo area.

A smaller pen had been created and inside petting zoo fence. Inside that pen was a small piglet. The instructions were clear, whoever went in the pen and caught the little piggy would be the grand prize winner. Some of the kids bowed out immediately, they didn't want to face the fearsome beast. I got in line and watched the first competitor tried to corner the piglet in the pen. I was up next, so I wanted to see if I could learn any strategies to capture the pig. The piglet was fast, and it easily ran through the legs of the apprehensive boy. He gave up after a few moments and then it was my turn.

I got into the pen, looking down on the creature I was determined to capture. I spread out my arms and legs and walked over like a crab, trying to make myself as much of a blockade as possible. I moved slowly as I approached the pig. Its back was turned, and it was pretending to not be paying attention as I approached. I pounced, taking hold of the back of the now squealing animal. I held it just above the back legs. It broke free from my grip after a quick wiggle. The pig's skin had left a thick residue on my hands and as I wiped it on my shirt the store owner spoke up.

"Oh, did I forget to mention that we greased up that pig." He explained with a huge smile.

The crowd laughed hard at the revelation that the animal is now going to be even harder to catch.

I reengaged with the pig and took another dive, just managing to grab a hind leg before it escaped again. After a third failed attempt, to snag the slippery creature, I gave up and let Nick into the pen.

Nick was quick and ran in the direction of the squirmy animal. He pounced, his body covering the entire pig. He wrapped his arms tightly around the middle of the pig and stood up. The legs of the screaming piglet were flailing about, angry from its departure from the ground.

"We have a winner!" the store owner cheered.

Nick put the pig back on the ground and it scurried away. Nick got out of the pen to claim his prize. Shaking his freshly buttered hands, trying to get off some stuck straw that clung to his fingers from the floor of pen. The store owner raised Nicks arm in triumph, and we all cheered.

Fred told the crowd of more snacks and chips that were setup near the barbeque, and we all cheered again. The group setoff to enjoy the rest of the afternoon. It was a great day playing next to the river.

Thomas Neamtu

The Iron Curtain

By the time eighth grade started I was starting to behave like a normal student. My disruptive behaviour was dwarfed by some of the other boys that had not yet found Mr. Latouche's enlightenment. Brent was one of these troublemakers, his antics quickly overshadowed mine and taught me some free lessons at his expense along the way.

Brent and I only shared a couple of classes together and the one where he would ramp up the shenanigans was in Ms. McGreggor's English class. She was not one of my favorite teachers, she had called my parents in for a meeting the year before. I was fortunate enough to have been forced to attend that bloodbath. The teacher didn't know my schoolwork apart from the other students, and she didn't even know where I sat in the classroom. Mom had been making sure that the work I needed to finish was getting done, so the accusations didn't sit well with her. I wasn't even asked to leave the room before mom ripped her a new one. That could have been the first sighting of moms alter ego, Frank Rizzo. After the meeting I was given a free pass in that class as my parents were no longer concerned about her opinions.

Roger had a similar situation, and his parents were called in for a parent teacher meeting. Ms. McGreggor had concerns about a story assignment Roger had turned in. The story had greatly upset the teacher and had even brought her to tears. She wanted Roger to be punished for the mental anguish and hurt that his story had caused. The tale in question was about a cute little piglet, Ms. McGreggor's favorite animal, that escaped from the farm and had a beautiful single day adventure. Roger laid the details on extra thick with sickening levels of cuteness. Ms. Mcgreggor fell in love with the tiny piglet. Roger concluded the story with the piglet meeting a gruesome death, and that conclusion broke the teacher. Ms. Mcgreggor wanted Roger to suffer for his personal attack. Rogers parents weren't having any of her concerns either and he too was given the pass from any of her future complaints.

The English class was at the end of the upstairs hallway, past the library and the computer lab. The room was divided by a corrugated temporary wall, turning the space into two equal sized rooms. The curtain would come out of a hole in the wall and stretch the length of the room. The bottom of the corrugated wall would sway as the students brushed up against it. Brent sat next to the moving wall and would be bumped occasionally as he worked on his reports. He would push back on the wall causing it to ripple like a stone in a pond. After a few more bumps Brent stood up from his desk and took a few steps back and charged at the wall. The wall lunged into the other classroom, knocking over the desk and sending the other unseen student to the ground. The wall wiggled and, in a few moments, settled back to its resting position. Brent returned to his seat and went back to work.

The teacher from the room next door rushed into our classroom expecting to find World War three, but we were all working quietly. Ms. McGreggor hadn't noticed the abrupt disruption to the wall and didn't know why the other teacher was standing in the door frame. Looking slightly confused the teacher returned to her class without comment, and we all giggled, knowing what had just happened.

For the next week every time Brent entered the room he would charge at the wall. you could hear the desks and chairs getting knocked over. He would try to get to class early so that the other room would be mostly vacant. Hitting an empty desk sent it careening across the room into other desks, messing up the tidy rows. His early arrival confused Ms. McGreggor as he was always in his seat before she arrived from her previous class, it was only down the hall at the computer lab.

After weeks of having the classroom in disarray the teacher from the other room wanted answers for why the desks were always upended. She arrived in her classroom early, to catch the culprit red handed. Sitting low in her desk, ducked behind a textbook to provide some extra cover, she waited for the vandal to walk in. Expecting an unruly student to come in and flip the desks and knock over the chairs. Her eyes were trained on the door, unblinking, her heart jumped, startled by the sudden movement in the classroom. She was surprised by the overturned desks and chairs, turning her attention to the far side of the class. The furniture slid on the short, grey carpet resting in the center of the room. She jumped from her seat looking around for the culprit who must have snuck in when she blinked. The room was completely empty, but the wall that divided the rooms was swaying, and in that instant, she knew what had been happening. Red faced and angry she stomped her way into our classroom. Half of the students were already in the room, and I had found my seat in the center desk of the back row. Three desks away from the wall.

"Who was it!?" she demanded.

Ms. McGreggor looking as clueless as ever. "Who was what?" she asked not knowing what the fiery outburst was for.

"Who keeps, knocking over all my desks!?" she demanded. "Who keeps banging into the wall, knocking over the chairs!?"

She interrogated wildly, looking around the room for the guilty party. All of us knew the answer to her heated questions, but we said nothing. Snitches get stitches. Our silence was met with more anger and a final ultimatum.

"Fine, this is the last time.!" She threatened. "If even one more chair gets bumped there will be hell to pay!" she turned and stomped out of our class.

Ms. McGreggor looked around shrugged her shoulders and asked rhetorically "I wonder what that was all about." Clueless.

The other class could hear the angry conversation through the wall. The dispute over the flexible divider and the ultimatum was too easy for some unpunishable chaos to be resisted. Some of the students laughed and decided that they would poke the bear and force some swinging wall retaliation to escalate the situation.

The rest of the day the wall was pushed from the other side, causing brent to lose his mind. Knowing that he was unable to enact the type of countermeasures required to win the battle of the iron curtain. He complained about being bumped and moved to a desk in the center of the room. His clever tactics were planned out, by not being near the epicenter of his next charge into the wall, he expected to not be blamed for the carnage.

Brent got up from his new seat and went to the front of the class to sharpen his pencil. He rotated the handle of the pencil sharpener until the length of the pencil had diminished a full inch. Satisfied that he had shown enough of a legitimate reason to be up from his seat, he returned towards his desk. As he got to the center of the wall, he faked a pratfall by tripping himself, pushing into the wall with both hands. Brent making a large spectacle of his clumsy footsteps. The force of the two-handed lunge into the wall, sent the unseen student to fall out of there desk onto the floor. Before Brent could even take his hands off the wall, the other teacher was in our classroom. She saw him standing next to the wall, before he could even make a lame excuse she stormed into the room and pulled him into the hallway by his arm.

Brent made loud vocal objections and tried to make jokes as he was forcefully removed from the classroom. Once they were both in the hall the teacher closed our door with more force than expected, causing it to slam loudly. We could hear through the walls the mumble of rage as Brent was read the riot act for his disruptive behavior. After what felt like an hour the door was opened by the teacher, she pulled Brent back into the awkwardly silent room. She Pointed at another student and directing them to move over to Brents desk, an objection wasn't even considered.

"You sit here now!" she said still angry directing Brent to his new seat in front of the teacher's desk.

"Ms. Mcgreggor will keep an eye on you from here." "If you so much as twitch, you will be sent to the principal's office! Understand!" she was looking for a confirmation.

Brent nodded his understanding but continued with the excuses, "it wasn't me!" "I think this room is haunted, a ghost pushed me into the wall."

The room giggled and the teacher shot her death ray vision around the room, reinstating the instant awkward silence. None of us were interested in catching any of her wrath over this transgression.

"It wasn't a ghost." She said turning her attention to Ms. Mcgreggor "keep a better eye on you students!" then stormed out of the classroom.

Brent said loudly from his new position of shame, "it was a ghost, it grabbed my ass" and the room laughed loudly, knowing better.

Having Brent sit in front of the teacher's desk was not the best plan. He was a troublemaker at heart and couldn't resist messing with Ms. Mcgreggor. She wasn't the sharpest knife in the drawer and that made her an easy target of his childish pranks. The tricks started small, like moving the items from the top of her desk and putting them in the unlocked drawers caused her hours of confusion. Even just hiding the stapler under the desk, took her days to find it.

Brent did manage to cross the line with a harmless trick that pushed her over the edge. He got to class before she did and dropped some rubber onto her chair. This went unnoticed by almost everyone, but I seen it happen. The class was about half full as the students wandered in and found their seats. Ms. Mcgreggor dropped some pages onto her desk, then moved to the front of the class to write on the black board. The class began on time, and she taught the English lesson. After thirty minutes of her chicken scratch on the blackboard, we were given our final instructions and asked to start the assignment. She walked back to her desk and took a seat. She had barely contacted the wooden chair before she was back on her feet, screaming. The shriek tore through the halls of the school and echoed in the library. The bloodcurdling howl was unnerving. The whole class sat at our desks with big eyes looking over at her bubbling meltdown. I seen Brent put something on the seat of her chair, but I had no idea what it was.

The librarian ran into the classroom to see who had died. The fifty feet traveled from the stacks of books had taken her breath away.

"What the hell is going on in here?" she said between hundred-year-old breaths.

"Look what they did." Ms. Mcgreggor said pointing to her chair, starting to sob, barely holding in the tears.

"What?" the librarian inquired, approaching the chair with caution.

"That!" Ms. Mcgreggor pointed, tears now running down her face, "the little monsters left vomit on my seat." She screeched. A flash of panic crossed her face. "Ah no, is it on me?" she said between weepy sobs.

The librarian picked up a pencil and went to poke at the offending addition to the chair. Brent jumped up to his feet unable to handle the guilt that he had just made the teacher cry, wanting to comfort her quickly.

"It's fake," he said quickly trying to calm down the situation. "Its not real, its only rubber."

Brent explained his joke as he went around the desk and picked up the rubber pad. It was a translucent rubber circle six inches in diameter designed to look like a puddle of fake puke. From my desk I could see a mix of peas, carrots and brown gravy.

The librarian was not impressed and told Brent to get to the principals' office. Brent left the room without any objection. The librarian then helped Ms. Mcgreggor out into the hallway so that she could regain her composure.

"Get a hold of your self," The librarian said kindly but firmly. "I though someone died," She explained. "I ran down the hall for some fake puke, ridiculous," She scolded the other teacher. "You better get control of these kids, or they will run you wild."

"Thanks, I'm better now." Ms. Mcgreggor said retracting her tears and wiping her cheeks. "I thought the mess was real, and I just lost it." She explained.

Starting to get embarrassed by her extreme reaction to a piece of rubber. She looked at the classroom door and the confidence drained from her face. The librarian noticed.

"Go rest in the library until the next period," the librarian instructed.

Ms. Mcgreggor nodded and started down the hallway to the quiet solitude of the library.

The librarian walked into the classroom still angry about what had happened.

"Finish your assignments, don't make a peep, if I have to come back down the hall you will all be getting detentions," She warned. She then went back to the library not even waiting for a response.

The class was silent for the remainder of the period, no one knowing how to react to what we had just witnessed. It might have been a funny prank if the teacher didn't cry, but the tears drained all the fun from the joke.

Part of Brents punishment was that he needed to make a public apology while standing at the front of the classroom. He was genuinely remorseful for his actions and vowed to be better. It sounded to me like he was brought into Mr.

Latouche's attitude adjustment program. After watching brent squirm at the front of the class for a few extra moments Ms. Mcgreggor accepted his apology, and we all went back to our scheduled lessons.

Brent was always the class clown but never pushed his antics that far again, he settled for random outbursts and fart noises.

Static White Noise

By grade nine I had my grades up and I was starting to participate in some of the school activities. I had made some lifelong friends and not letting them down was more important than fighting the system. I still broke the rules every day, but I got my assignments in on time.

At lunch we would play football in the field behind the school. The turf was far enough away from the building that the teachers didn't wander by very often, and we were left out there on our own. The school had no rules against playing football, only if there was no physical contact, but we never played by the rules. We would knock each other over, pushing and shoving to get possession of the undersized football. The smaller ball made it easier to throw and harder to catch. We would spend the lunch hour running around, tossing the ball and having a good time.

After a few weeks we collectively decided that more players were needed to have a football serious game. We all went out to recruit some of the larger eighth grade students. Not a single kid from the grade eight class was willing to come out to play against us. So, we needed to adjust our search parameters and tried to find the kids in the seventh grade that had a little bit of spine.

We found a few that were willing to play, excited to be included into the group of older students. With the addition we finally had enough players to have seven kids on each team and we played some epic games. The teams were set, and we all played against the same grouping everyday. At lunch we would assemble and battle over the ball for a vicious half hour. The younger kids were just as tough and never backed down, playing hard every day.

My first period after lunch was always an hour of quiet reading. I would sit in my desk and the wet grass would fall from my jeans as it dried. The moist grass and leaves collecting in a messy pile under my seat. My pants were always saturated with field water from the knees down, the sticky denim cold against my hairy legs. The smell of the field would follow me for the rest of the day. The sweet stench of field water. The other players in my class would depart from the reading hour with similar messes under there desks. The teacher was not impressed at our daily redistribution of wet leaves and dirt.

As the season went on the games got more physical and intense. What would normally have been just a push was now turned into a shove. The trash talking was escalating between the plays and the fight for victory was starting to be treasured above one's own wellbeing.

I was tossed the ball and was running down the sideline when I was tackled by Matt. I was knocked over and Matt landed on top of me. I stretched out my right arm to brace my body from the fall. The extra weight of Matt on top of me causing me to land harder than expected. Matt stood up first and offered me an outstretched hand. We battled hard against each other every day at lunch but were good friends off the field.

"Good run," he said pulling me up from the ground.

"Thanks, I almost made it." I said, as I stood up.

I got to my feet and felt a bit dizzy. I adjusted my footing, so I didn't fall over.

"Are you alright?" Matt asked concerned about my balance.

"I don't think so, I might have sprained my wrist," I explained.

I could tell right away that something wasn't right. The vision out of my right eye was being funny. The shadows on the ground were replaced with a black and white static like that on an out of service channel on a television. My brain was trying to do a damage report, and my static vision was the result.

"I did smash you pretty good," Matt said with a cheeky smile, "Let me help you to the nurse."

We walked off the field and went towards the office. Matt had his arm around my shoulder helping me to balance my walk. We joked as we walked back towards the school. I had helped Matt to the nurse's office the week before. He had bumped heads with another player and had split open an eyebrow. The seventh-grade cowboy was unfazed but the collision and stayed out on the field to finish the game. When I helped Matt back to the school the blood flowed down his face, dripping down his chin. He laughed maniacally as we moved down the hallway to the office, more upset about the deep stain on his shirt than the dripping head wound. Matt needed a few stitches over his eye, but never complained about anything other than his shirt.

Once we were in the office I went to see the nurse. She was not happy to see the pair of us again. I began telling her how we were playing a gentile game of football, and I think that I had sprained my wrist. She gave it a quick wiggle and I winced in pain. It didn't hurt much, but any quick direction changes to my wrist made me grimace. She agreed that it was probably just a sprain and wrapped a tension bandage around my sore wrist. The lunch bell had sounded while I was being bandaged, so we were directed back to class.

I went home and showed mom the bandage and explained what had happened at lunch. She took a quick look and using the bedside manor of a mad scientist told me that I was alright, and that I would survive. The next morning, I was sent back to school with a fresh tension bandage. Its tight wrap providing comfort to the demobilized wrist. As the day progressed the wrist became more inflamed and had started to swell. My arm was starting to throb, as the blood forced its way past the bandage. I toughed it out until the end of the day, not wanting to miss a single moment of shop class, even if my arm might have fallen off.

In Shop class we were working on our wooden cars and that was the biggest project of the year. The goal was to take a piece of wood that was shaped like a wedge, modify it down to a more aerodynamic shape using the guidelines. There were guidelines to follow as to how much you could take from the original piece, so each car would fit into some sort of standard. Then plastic wheels would be attached, a hole would be drilled in the back. The hole in the back would hold a small carbon dioxide canister that upon puncture would propel the constructed car forward. The wood blocks on wheels would race the length of the classroom to see who had constructed the fastest design. I was still working on thinning out the center between the front wheels and the canister. There were only a few more weeks left until race day, and I wanted to finish strong, so missing any shop time was unacceptable.

Returning home that night I had my mother help remove the bandage. My arm had turned a deep purple and had swelled up substantially. I had found out in shop class that I was unable to put any pressure on the tips of my fingers. Demonstrating to my mom with a can of soda. I was unable to pickup the red can of sugar water, not being able to get any hold or grip with my fingertips. Mom took a second look at my mismatched arm and decided we should go to the clinic to see if anything more severe than a sprain had occurred.

The clinic was down by the corner store and only took a few minutes to get to. In that time my arm had gotten even bigger. We only had to wait a few moments before we were shown into an examination room. The doctor followed in behind us. I was asked to put my arm on the table, so a widened my stance and leaned into the paper covered examination table. I laid my arm down with care as the cold paper crinkled. The doctors' warm hands caressed the swelling joint with probing fingers. The pokes and prods didn't hurt as I was asked how each touch felt. Then the doctor gave my arm a twist, and my feet left the ground. I pulled my arm to my chest, with pain in my face and anger in my eyes I barked out my displeasure. We were then told that x-rays would probably be required and were then instructed to go to the hospital to have the radioactive pictures taken. We thanked the doctor half-heartedly and went off towards the hospital. My arm hurting worse than when I first arrived at the clinic.

We checked in at the hospital and were told to have a seat in the waiting room. Mom and I got comfortable after being told that waiting for x-rays could take some time. The waiting room was filled with lots of people that all needed more attention than I did. I wasn't going to die at that exact moment, but some of them might have. One guy across from us looked like he was dragged behind a car. His arms and chest were full of stones, and he was making a low pitch guttural whine. We were happy when the nurses took him away to be looked after, returning the waiting rooms' volume back to the standard roar of people suffering. Mom and I joked that if we wanted to be seen by a doctor sooner, I should start screaming like a banshee, but it didn't need to come to that, as we were collected shortly after by the nurse that check us in.

We went into the examination room, and I was instructed again to put my arm on the cold, serialized table. The table was a cold stainless steel, the cool temperature felt good on my swollen flesh. I had my arm in the most comfortable position I could manage, resting on the shined-up steel. The nurse pulled my arm forward; to line up with the machine, this caused me to let out a yelp of discomfort. She asked me to rotate the arm slightly so that the machine could get a picture of the bone from the desired angle. I was unable to make this request as my arm had stopped listening to my commands. The nurse took hold of my arm with her warm but not gentile hands and twisted it into the desired position. I let out another yelp as she realigned the arm to the aligned position. I was given quick instructions not to move as a heavy led vest was draped over my shoulders. The nurse quickly left the room. I loud beep emanated from over my head and the nurse returned to pull off the weighted vest. Mom and I were then sent to another examination waiting room, away from the new patients that were still ready to be admitted.

The doctor arrived soon after with the x-ray picture in his hands. I was told that I had a fracture just above my wrist and that I was going to need a cast. He said that a nurse would be around to put on the plaster. A new nurse arrived just as the doctor was walking out of the room. I was given the choice of the standard white plaster cast, or one made of blue fiberglass. I chose the blue one. She wrapped my arm with more care and precision than the x-ray technician. And after a few short minutes the cast was secured on my arm, and we were sent on our way.

Six Lives Left

I returned to school on Friday with my new bone adjusting fashion accessory. My friends were surprised at the new addition, not expecting that my arm was broken. I was going to be stuck with this blue cast for the next six weeks. The cast didn't stop me from playing football at lunch, it actually made for a pretty good bludgeon, keeping the other players away.

I didn't let the cast slow me down in anyway, I was still training for the upcoming bike trip. The cast was scheduled to come off a few weeks before we would depart on that mountain adventure.

At the end of year school assembly, I was called up onto the stage at the front of the gym and presented an award for perfect attendance. There were a bunch of academic awards, but the one I received was held with the highest regard, because even with a broken arm I didn't miss a single day of school. I'd like to see a brainiac nerd try that one. It might be the last time that award has ever been handed out. Kids nowadays get to stay home from school for having hurt feelings, I went days with broken bones. The cheer from the audience as I walked up on stage to collect the engraved brass plaque filled my heart with joy. I collected the award and got off stage as quickly as possible, not wanting to be center of attention for a second longer than necessary. I was happy to be acknowledged but I wasn't looking for any admiration. The award was a nice finish to the school year and setup a positive transition to high school. Most of the kids that I was currently going to class with were planning to attend the other high school, so I wouldn't see most of them again anyway. But the cheers as I walked off the stage were energizing and much appreciated.

Thomas Neamtu

Bike Trip 1995 – The Beginning

I had signed up to participate in the schools' annual bike trip that was championed by our math teacher. I rode my bike every day anyway and looked forward to the potential of a new challenge.

Fish creek park was full of a variety of paths, and I tried to be out there every possible moment of the day. The smooth and effortless glide of my bike's robust tires over the park's pavement was starting to get old. I wanted to face the next challenge, the Rocky Mountains. Our teacher gave out the prospective participating students a sheet with the challenge goal of five thousand kilometers, due before the trip's departure. This would request would prove the worthiness and commitment to the bike team. The assignment was due in three months, I felt that that was plenty of time to finish the task. The required fifty kilometres a day was easily met, as I would ride an eighty-kilometre circuit around the city twice a week. Calgary has one of the best path systems in the world and we used it to full potential.

Six Lives Left

Halfway through the bike training I broke my arm playing football at lunch. The blue cast made it hard to stretch my hand over the brake on the handlebar, but I never slowed down anyway, always pushing to go faster.

The cast did happen to come in handy on one occasion. It was a Saturday; I was riding alone. I had just about finished the city circuit and just crossed the final bridge over the river, starting in on the home stretch. There was a misplaced rock from the river on the yellow painted centerline of the divided path. Someone must have pulled the football sized stone from the water and abandoned it on the pavement. I noticed it late and was on top of it before I reacted. I had been out riding for the last four hours and was lost in a daydream about the nachos I was going to have when I got home. My eyes locked on the path further up the trail. Once I noticed the eminent impact with the stone, I pulled up on the handlebar.

My front tire lifted from the ground and skipped over the rock. The back tire bounced off the stone as my front tire stood tall in the air. I rode six feet past the rock with the front tire held above the ground. When the front tire of the bike made its decent back towards the paved trail, the wheel fell off the forks. The bolt that held the tire in place must have been loose, the impact from the rock, knocking the loose nut free. My mind slowed down time, as I watched the front tire roll away without me. I watched as my front forks made grinding contact with the ground, stopping my forward momentum instantly. Tossing me off the bike, over the handlebar. Instinctively I put my arm out in front of my face. The casted arm took all the damage and prevented me from scraping the skin from my chin. I got up from the ground quickly not wanting to have others see my embarrassing accident. I walked over and retrieved the wayward tire, returning it to the bike, reattaching it to the forks. I twisted the bolt back into position as best I could, tuning the nut until it was snug. I remounted the bike and continued home for my dreamed-up salsa and chips. I inspected the cast as I rolled towards home, it had taken a deep impact and looked like a belt sander had taken out a jagged stripe. The blue coating of the cast was replaced by a scrapped up white underbelly of criss-crossed mesh. The damaged cast was due to come off in a few more days anyway, so I wasn't too concerned of its overall condition. My arm didn't sustain any more injury, it must have been mostly healed by that point anyhow. I was glad that I had some blue armor to protect me from the damage I would surely have gotten from the pavement.

I handed in my required milage sheets three weeks early and was amped up about the upcoming departure. The trip was from Jasper to Banff. Two hundred and eighty-eight kilometers of mountain riding, over three challenging days. There were planned out camping spots along the way. The daily goals of the required distance would get us to our sleeping bags and flimsy mostly water-resistant tents. It was going to be epic, and I could hardly wait.

Bike Trip 1995 – Day One

I got dropped off at the school at the crack of dawn, the crisp morning air only invigorated me more for the upcoming journey. It was strange being at the school just after sunrise. I pulled my bike out of the trunk of Dads car, making sure not to let the bungee cord recoil into my chilly fingers. I told my parents farewell, and they wished me luck on the three-day excursion. I gathered my sleeping bag and backpack. Then pushed my bike over to the waiting truck to have it loaded into the cube van that was taking all the supplies up to Jasper. Everyone's bikes would be stacked in with the camping supplies and food for the three-day adventure. Having done the trip for years there were some extra bike parts, spare tire tubes and bike chains just in case someone had a blow out or snapped a chain. The teachers had learned some hard lessons from past trips and now travelled prepared for quick onsite repairs. I had my own chain links packed inside my bike pouch and had gotten quite proficient at replacing snapped chain pins. My legs had gotten strong and when climbing up steep hills I would snap the bike chain often.

The bike team all boarded the bus and waived goodbye to our parents as they lingered on the grass in the front of the school. I'm sure most of the parents just wanted to see the taillights disappear around the corner, so that they knew for certain that we had departed for the seventy-two hours of childless bliss.

The bus was loud with the chatter of excited students, I could feel the energy building inside. We were all energized to get our bike rolling on the highway, but we had a four-and-a-half-hour bus ride to survive first. After an hour of travel the bus started to quiet down, as we all began to concentrate on the physical battle we were about to take on, getting our minds focused on the challenges ahead. I turned on my tape player, closed my eyes and drifted off to sleep, dreaming of our soon to be adventure.

The bus pulled into the shaded courtyard. The roar of enthusiasm disrupted the silence of the parking lot as we all disembarked from the bus. Cheering loudly about or future glory, as we stretched out our cramped muscles from the long ride. I walked down the steps of the charted bus and into the cold morning mountain air, stretching my anxious legs. The van had arrived in Jasper not long before the bus, it had time to get all the bikes unloaded before we arrived. The bikes were all lined up orderly with all of them facing the same direction. The handlebars were staggered with our helmets hanging from the grips. The team wandered over and stood next to the bikes, giving them a quick inspection. I pulled out my riding gloves from my backpack and put them on. The smell of the leather was comforting as I stretched over the Velcro strap, locking the gloves to my hands.

Mr. Leavens called for our attention, and we turned to face him and the other teacher chaperone Miss Kuss. Mr. Leavens then proceeded to give us a rousing speech of encouragement.

"Today we start out on our epic adventure," he began. "And by the time we ride the hundreds of kilometres through these beautiful mountains, you will have accomplished something most people will never even attempt." He took a pause for effect. "Just knowing that you were able to complete such an incredible feat, will push you further in life." He paused again, "knowing for certain that you will be able to accomplish anything that the future sends your way." "Because you will all be strong in the knowledge that you conquered these mountains, and no one can take that away from you, ever!" Mr. Leavens finished strong, "Now, lets ride!" He shouted raising a fist to the sky.

We all cheered in unison; fists raised to the sky. Mr. Leavens turned towards Miss Kuss to see if she had anything to add, but the attention was lost as we all mounted our bikes eager to start the ride after his inspirational speech.

The bike team set off on the journey. The first leg of the trip was a meager seventy kilometers to the first campground. That distance was less than my normal ride, so I wasn't too worried. I waited for the bulk of the students to take off before following, not wanting to be caught up in an early bottle neck of riders. I had been training for months and my body was ready to take on these mountain roads. I stepped onto the bike pedal as it rotated towards the ground. The bike rolled with ease and as every great journey begins with a single step, ours had just begun.

Right away you could tell who handed in falsely adjusted milage reports, heavy breathing and slow pace was an immediate give away. I rode past the weaker riders without breaking stride. On the flatter ground I was making up distance quickly on the riders ahead of me. I would pass them all on the short hills and steeper inclines. I trained hard for months, the largest of the gears that provided resistance on my bike were the only ones I ever used. The moment I noticed the person in front of me gear down to climb up a hill, I would just pump my legs a little harder, passing them with ease. As some of the others struggled with the climb, gearing down into a smaller granny gear, I would just keep my knees pumping and pass by them all. By the time I reached the crest of the first real hill I was behind just the teacher.

Mr. Leavens was riding a road bike with precariously thin tires, that gave him the advantage of very little road surface to cause resistance to his strides. The thin tires did come at a cost, a rock or branch would be dangerous to ride over, not having much room for error. My bike had the standard, wide mountain bike tires. I had more resistance from the treads sure, but I could traverse almost anything that was in the road. His bike took less energy to climb the steep inclines, but I had stubborn willpower and had trained hard to meet the physical requirements needed to thrive. Once we were at the top of the first major incline, the teacher and I waited for the others to catch up. I used this time to have a quick power bar for a snack to regain some energy.

When the last riders huffed there way to meet with the rest of us, the teacher called for a return to the road, with a ten-minute warning. This would give the stragglers a chance to consume some calories and have a short, yet well-deserved rest. I was ready to go, I had been resting for half an hour. Once the group was ready to depart again, I waited for them to disperse before following, knowing that I would be back at the front of the pack before long.

After a few hours riding on the mountain road we arrived at the first camp, marmot meadows. The supply truck was running late, and we ended up waiting for its arrival. The cube van had all the camping gear and food, so we couldn't get started on setting up the camp until it arrived. Once it showed up, we laid out all the camping gear on the grass. I found a tent and went to set it up. I chose a spot in the designated area near the woods. Some of the tents went up quicker than others, but it didn't take long until we had a little tent city built along the edge of the trees.

As we waited for dinner to be sorted out, we all sat around and bickered over the miles we had traveled. Stories of animal sightings filled the conversations. Dinner was called and we rushed over to consume some burnt hotdogs. As the sun set on our first night out, we sat around the campfire trying to keep warm and roast some marshmallows. The stories grew more outrageous as the night wore on, but it was all in good fun.

Everyone was tired and ready to try and have as good of a sleep as possible, as good as sleeping on the ground could be anyway. The fire was extinguished and we all retreated to our prepared tents. I crawled into my waiting sleeping bag and tried to fall asleep quickly, worried that the nearby tents had snoring occupants. I tossed and turned until I removed the rock that was protruding from the ground under my sleeping bag. I then found a deep slumber until the morning sunrise when the camp returned to life.

Bike Trip 1995 – Day Two

The tent city was disassembled and packed away in the truck before we had breakfast. We had a quick morning meal of burnt toast and flavorless cereal. The conversation turned heated when one of the girls asked Mr. Michelles why he slept in the truck over night and not in the tent that he had setup.

"A what?" she screeched.

"A black bear, this big," He informed her of the bear sighting, starching out his arms to exaggerate the animal's size. "I'm not taking any chances."

"Well, that's not fair, what about the rest of us." She interrogated.

She was mad because, we could have all been in danger from the wandering beast, if it even existed. Mr. Michelles continued to tease her growing concern, which leads me to believe there was never even a bear in the campground.

"I didn't have to outrun the bear just you." He said with a cheeky grin and a pointing finger.

We all laughed as she pouted at the thought of being a midnight snack for a bear.

Once breakfast was choked down and the dirty dishes were cleaned up, we mounted our bikes and began the second days journey. This leg of the trip was the longest with just under a hundred kilometres to travel. Mr. Michelles would follow behind the group of bike riders after he packed up the rest of the gear. He would keep enough distance between the last of the riders to be available if anyone had a breakdown.

I took up my late departure positions and followed behind the pack. I took our time and didn't rush to the first checkpoint. The morning ride took an hour, before we stopped for rest at the base of the mountain we would soon need to climb. The team was informed that the next four kilometers were going to be the steepest incline we would encounter, as we rode up through the Sunwapta pass. This was going to be the most challenging part of the trip. There was a level rest area about two thirds of the way up and we would take a scheduled break at that point. After a group cheer of mixed enthusiasms, we started up the mountain pass.

Once the group started to spread out, I followed. Systematically passing each rider, as they were gasping and digging deep to find the power to push on, I passed with a wave and a smile. The bell on the handlebar dining my intentions as I passed on the left. My lungs were burning as the highway leveled out and the clearing approached. Mike had passed me way back, but I was making up some ground. We were going to be the first two at the top with Mr. Leavens, whose road bike made the climb look easy. He took the grade nine students on this trip every year and was well conditioned to handle the excruciating climb. My legs were on fire from the thousands of peddle rotations it took to get to the top. The burning muscles were a nice reminder that I was having fun.

Mike and I made it to the top and found a quick snack. Standing off to the side of the road next to the guard rail, as Mr. Leavens pulled out the camcorder to document the arrival of the other students. He was making a video to commemorate the trip and capture some of the highlights of the adventure. Mike and I were eating our tasteless power bars as the next riders reached the summit.

"Hey girls, how does it feel to be the first ones to the top of the mountain?" He asked with excitement.

"Just happy to be alive." The one answered.

Mr. Leavens panning the camera as the girls passed him, showing Mike and I standing next to the guard rail eating our flavorless snacks, clearly the first to get to the summit. It wasn't a race, but we were there first, for the record. Once the whole group was gathered at the plateau we rested for a few more minutes before continuing up to the top. We all took another rest once we reached the top after another punishing hour of burning lungs and twitching thighs.

The climb up the mountain pass was a full battle of will. I kept my head down, focused only on the road in front of me. My hat poking out from under my helmet keeping the view up the mountain limited to only twenty feet in front of me. The cracked pavement sliding by as I pushed on. My legs pumped with pain every rotation of my peddles, testing my resolve every second of the journey. The strategy was to make small distance goals and after achieving the small victory, push on to the next one. The reward at the top would be a sandwich bag full of trail mix, sorted with nuts, coconut and small chunks of chocolate. With every forced stride I let my mind wander, letting my body find its rhythm as I approached towards the days ultimate victory.

Once at the top I took a well-deserved rest and let the fire burn out of my lungs. My mouth was dry, from the miles of breathing in the mountain air. The first gulp of fresh water from the refilled coolers soothed my burning throat, instantly providing a much-needed rejuvenation. I stood next to the guard rail with Mike. Each of us breathing heavy, as we let our heartrates return to normal after pushing our bodies to the absolute limit. It had been an excruciating climb and now we got to enjoy the view.

Miss Kuss wandered by with the video camera looking for some words of wisdom. At that moment I had nothing to share, being a man of very few words. Mike tried to toss his half-eaten power bar over the rail and into the wilderness but was dissuaded by Miss Kuss of such actions. She was scared a squirrel would eat the power bar and be so upset by the flavorless human treat. Then the squirrel would vow vengeance, going on a killer squirrel rampage, out for human blood. Her concern was more likely she just didn't want us to chuck garbage into the wilderness.

After everyone was rehydrated and somewhat rested, we were given a congratulatory speech for reaching one of highest points of our journey at over six thousand six hundred and seventy feet above sea level. We all let out a victorious cheer at our conquest. We were then told the next leg of the journey was all downhill. The next nine kilometers were all a downward descent. Departures of the riders were going to be staggered by thirty seconds; this was deemed to be enough time for the rider behind to react if any misfortune fell on riders up front. Mike and I didn't wait to be last this time around and moved up towards the front of the line, anxious to be back on the road.

With fresh legs I crested the hill and enjoyed the quick descent down the winding highway. The decline went on for further than I could see, the winding road only providing limited visibility on the upcoming terrain. I pumped my legs hard, trying to get the maximum amount of speed. I had no more gears on my bike to increase the resistance and maxed out my top speed at around seventy kilometers an hour. The riders in front of me, keeping a furious pace, were unable to be caught, all pushing for top speed.

The wide shoulder on the highway was filled with cracks and missing chunks of pavement so a keen awareness was needed as I ripped down the mountain. The adrenaline was different than the climb and I enjoyed it as the endorphins pumped through my veins. The winding road forcing my attention to stay in the moment. The weather turned into a misty rain that collected on my glasses, fogging up my already limited vision. The coolness of the fresh moisture felt good as it soaked into my already wet and sweaty clothes.

The full decent ended at bow summit. The ground was covered with a fresh snow from the night before. The air was colder at the bottom of the mountain and pulled at my wet clothes, forcing steam to rise from my shoulders. Soon we would be at the next camp, excited to have an individual homemade pizza for dinner. The team pushed on and rolled into the designated campground a short while later. The tent city was setup with haste, taking less time than the day before.

After finding some warm, dry clothes, we all crammed into the camps kitchen and made our own pizzas; the excitement of making a warm meal filled the room. The premade dough was smothered with a bright red tomato sauce, then covered in a few basic pizza ingredients, and topped with a pre-shredded cheese. The final product was terrible, possibly the worst pizza in the history of the world, but we were hungry and that made the meal fantastic. No one complained about the burnt edges or mediocre quality, we were all just happy to be eating. The room was loud with the tales of the day. There were a few almost disastrous moments on the road and those stories were old with maximum amounts of exaggeration, to add effect.

The group chatter continued well after the meal finished. We all gathered around in the kitchen as the sun went down. At some point in the evening, we all had to move to the front of the room and tell something about ourselves, or a piece of advice. This was moderated by Miss Kuss, and she called on each of us, in a random order.

When I was called upon, I went to the front of the room.

Miss Kuss asked, "Thomas, do you have any words of wisdom that you would like to share?"

I didn't have any spring to mind at that moment. She noticed my hesitation and moved on quickly.

"Tell us about the dinosaur tooth." She said, pointing to the one hanging around my neck.

I took the friendly nudge and answered "Hello, this is the replica dinosaur tooth that I had purchased at the lake Luise gift shop." I said, lifting the leather string that held it around my neck.

The tooth garnered some positive attention as I dropped the string, and the casted tooth returned to the original position hung from my neck. I didn't like all the attention directed to me and quickly returned to my spot in the back after saying very little.

The others gave their comical wisdom and advice to the group to laughs and cheers. The girls gave warnings after their tent was being peed on the night before, the room filled with laughter at the childish prank. Other memorable words of wisdom involved peeing on a glacier and the infinite wonders of duct tape. After an hour of collected laugher we all went to our tents to have some well-deserved sleep after a long day.

Thomas Neamtu

Bike Trip 1995 – Day Three

I woke up at sunrise to another quick cereal breakfast, anxious to get back on the road and finish up the last leg of the journey. The idea of not spending another night sleeping on the ground was great motivation to get home. Today the ride was going to be relatively easy compared to the challenges faced on the day before. The sun was out, and the cloudless blue mountain sky was encouraging as the group started to peddle our way towards Banff.

These were three of the best days ever, the hard work, and preparation had paid off. The bike team had all achieved something that most people would never even try to attempt, and that accomplishment was to be cherished. Just knowing that I never gave up, when my legs screamed, and my lungs burned. Quitting would have been easy, but not giving up fills me with great satisfaction and pride even now. The words from Mr. Leavens rousing speech from the first day ringing true.

The last days ride was an enjoyable scenic tour. The bright blue sky provided the perfect backdrop for the mountainous terrain. I rode past waterfalls and millions of trees. The pain from the day before drifting away memory as we got closer to town. The wilderness rejuvenating my body and spirit, as the fresh mountain air filled my lungs. This had been a once in a lifetime experience and I was starting to feel the significance.

The team got into town and rode to the designated pickup location. The bikes were all loaded into the truck for safe transport home. We had some time before the bus was scheduled to leave. The group took this time to wander around some of the shops, looking for treasures, before boarding the bus back to school. I had got my dinosaur tooth a few days earlier and was satisfied with my memento.

The ride home was filled with stories of the adventure. Some of the girls almost got run off the road by a disgruntled big horn sheep. They told the tale of there near miss encounter with big grins and exaggerated hand movements, making sure we all knew how big the animal was and how close they had come to a destructive impact. We were all champions that day! We had conquered the mountains! Each of us had survived our own quest of strength and will power, to finish off the two hundred eighty-eight-kilometer test of endurance. I hope everyone of the participants remember those three days as fondly as I do. (If you ever want to see that replica dinosaur tooth, I can show it to you, and if you ask nicely, I might even let you hold it.)

We got back to the school to our parents waiting for us, standing on the same grass as when we first departed. I was glad to be back home, longing for a hot shower and a warm meal. The bike team disembarked the bus and dispersed quickly, as everyone was excited to be home and excited to tell of the adventure

My parents took me home to drop off my gear, then we went out for dinner. They were excited to hear all the details of the adventure. Over a steaming hot lasagna, I told them of my triumph. The lasagna disappeared in a few bites and Dad jokingly asked if I wanted another. The second lasagna disappeared just as quickly as the first, as I continued to tell of all the animal sightings. We left for home, and I was ready for a good night sleep in a soft, warm bed, not worrying about any new miles that needed to be traveled the next day. Bike Trip ninety-five was a great success and I would recommend anyone to give it a try, if they want to see what they are made of. It's a true test of will and mental endurance.

Door Damage

It was almost a regular Tuesday. I had gym class for first period and was excited to get some physical activity early in the day. I walked down the hall with the rest of the students rushing to their first class. Hubert was walking in front of me as we moved down the hall. He passed through the doors that separated the library from the rest of the upstairs classrooms. Just as the door was closing, Hubert planted his foot behind the base of the door, preventing it from opening fully. I pushed through the door with speed and was met with sudden stop, as the door only opened halfway. I could see him through the wired glass of the door smiling at his morning trickery.

The frame of my glasses clipping the edge of the door, biting into the soft skin above my eyebrow. With the sudden smack to my face my hand instinctively investigated the furry caterpillar above my eye. My fingers came back sticky and red, covered in the fresh blood from above my left eye. Hubert looked sacred as he unblocked the door and rushed away to the downstairs locker room. I followed him down the hallway, then down the stairs to the main floor.

I had my hand pressed against the eyebrow, stopping the flow of blood from fresh cut. My glasses were bent, the left arm was resting on the outside of my ear. Hubert went into the locker room, I followed with an outstretched arm, to prevent the door from making a repeat performance. He moved on towards the lockers and I stopped at the bathroom mirror to assess the damage. I pulled my hand away cautiously, a fresh flow of blood stained down my face. I had a one inch cut running parallel with my left eyebrow, blood was flowing out rapidly, dripping from my chin. I wet a paper towel and held it to the damage above my eye with my left hand. I used another towel to tidy up my face as it was covered with the beginnings of a crimson mask. Once I was satisfied with the results of a quick clean up, I left the bathroom and went to the main office for assistance. I walked up to the receptionist and told her that I needed a Band-Aid.

"I think I need a Band-Aid." I said forcing a smile.

"The day just started, what could have happened already?" she asked questioning the requirement for first aid.

I reluctantly removed my hand holding the wet paper towel from my face and watched as the color drained from hers. The blood trickled instantly down my cheek. I returned the towel to the wound and stopped the blood flow again.

"You are going to need stitches, for sure." She said as she braced herself on the counter. "We better call you mom."

"You can't!" I said with a mater of fact tone.

"Why not?" she asked concerned. "You're not in any kind of trouble," she said with reassurance.

"Mom's not home on Tuesdays, its her golf league lady's day." I explained.

She nodded and pulled out my file, looking for my fathers' work number to make the call to him. I was instructed to have a seat and wait as she called my father to come get me. I tried to fix my glasses as I waited but the arm was more damaged than I could adjust with only one hand. As I waited in the uncomfortable office chairs, Hubert popped his head in the office door and apologized for the accident. I assured him I was going to be fine and that there were no hard feelings. He rushed away back to gym class, as I waited for my dad.

Hubert was a funny kid. He lived at the bottom of our street and had only moved in just as school year started. His family had come from Poland, and he was the only one who spoke English. His stories of his homeland were intriguing. Poland was mostly the same as here, but the differences were interesting to learn about. Hubert had a little brother, probably four years old, he was not quite old enough to go to school yet. The brother was a cute kid other than he was missing his two front teeth. This gave him a look of menace when he grinned his big toothless smile. The little brother would play out in the front yard waving to everyone. He really was a friendly little guy. Hubert being a fellow troublemaker had taught his little brother that "hello" was "fuck you." That happy toothless kid greeted every person that passed by his yard with an enthusiastic welcome. Huberts little brother almost gave the poor old lady at the end of the street a heart attack when they met on the property divide.

"Well, hello, are you not just the most precious thing I ever seen." She greeted with a warm elderly smile.

Hubert's brother smiled back, his grin stretching all the way to the corners of his eyes. His warm smile beaming back all toothless and gummy. "Fuck you," he greeted happily.

The color drained from her face, and she rushed away from the child upset by the interaction.

Huberts's brother was confused by the sudden change in her affections and chased after her. His short arm waiving as he shouted his profanity, trying to regain her attention with no luck. He went home saddened by the interaction and was comforted by his mother who didn't know any better.

Later in the day the sweet old lady went back over to their house and informed the parents of the interaction. The old lady wanted to make sure that she got her message across and that it wasn't lost in translation. She told the new Canadians that their child was confused about his greetings and managed to get her point across using hand signals, and a middle finger. Once the parents understood that his "hello" was the same as a middle finger Hubert had some explaining to do. He was grounded for a few weeks and didn't want to have any more days added for our unfortunate morning accident.

Dad arrived at the school a short time later to take me to the clinic back in the neighborhood to have my eyebrow gash looked at. He had just made it to his office when the call came in about my incident. Dad walked into the school and got me from the receptionist, we departed without a word. Once we got back to the car dad started with the jokes.

"There are easier ways to get out of class," dad said with a cheeky smile. "What even happened?" "How do you get hurt before school even starts?" He questioned the circumstances of the accident.

I retold him of the braced door and showed him my bent glasses. He shook his head, and we continued to the clinic listening to the traffic report on the radio.

Dad parked the car in the spot directly in front of the doctor's office. We went up to the door of the clinic together. Dad gave it a hearty tug and the door didn't move. It was still locked; the clinic didn't open until nine. We had over half an hour wait before my head wound could be examined. Dad looked over his shoulder and turned around, the club house for the golf course was across the street.

"Let's go get some breakfast while we wait." He suggested as he started to walk off the sidewalk.

"Sounds good to me," I said with excitement.

We crossed the parking lot, then the street, walking over to the golf course restaurant. The restaurant was empty as all the golfers had departed for their rounds. The remnants of the pregame were evident by the half-finished coffee mugs scattered on the vacant tables. We chose a table that was freshly tidied and was instantly greeted by the friendly waitress.

We didn't need menus and ordered our second breakfast. Dad got his coffee, and I had my chocolate milk. By the time our beacon and eggs arrived my wound had stopped bleeding. The paper towel was now dried up and rusty.

As we finished our meal, I tried to talk my way out of going back over to the clinic. Dad refused my pleas as he paid for the breakfast. We then walked back to the now open doctor's office. We were the first and only patients in the waiting room, so we were directed straight into the examination room. I sat on the paper covered table and waited for the doctor to arrive.

"Good morning," the doctor greeted, her breath smelling of fresh coffee. "What do we have here on this fine day." She asked rhetorically as she pulled her wheeled chair into position in front of me.

I pointed to my eyebrow and pulled off my crooked glasses so she could get a better look.

"I lost a fight with a door," I said with a sheepish smile.

"Well, its good that the bleeding stopped, but I think we should still get you a couple of stitches anyway," She explained. "Three or four should do it, that way the scar will be less noticeable."

Before I could make any objection and tell her that chicks dig scars, she reached up and ripped off the newly formed scab. I flinched as the dried blood and eyebrow hairs were pulled from my face. The cut instantly started to pour blood down the side of my face. She caused more pain and gore while I sat on the examination table then the original incident. I was not very happy as she pulled out the needle and thread to stitch me back up to stop the bleeding that was already previously under control.

After a few minutes of watching her hand holding the needle as it approached my eye, then diverting up at the last possible second, the ordeal was finished. I was patched up and ready to go back to school. Luckily not needing an eye patch or any other ridiculous bandage. I thanked her for the unnecessary stitches and went outside the examination room, back to the front entrance. Dad stopped at the receptionists' counter to see if we would need a follow up appointment. I went outside to wait by the car.

The car doors were unlocked, and I took a seat inside and waited for dad to come out. Once dad was back in the car I asked to go home and get a new shirt, as mine was now covered in blood.

"That's probably a good idea," he said. "She really did a number on you."

"Thanks, you're not kidding," I said, "the stitches hurt more than the fight with the door." I joked with a chuckle.

Dad took me home for a quick shirt change then back to school where I finished out the day with four stitches holding in my blood. Dad dropped me off in front of the school and departed with some words of wisdom and a warning that he wouldn't be back if I got hurt again. I reassured him of a second injury not being an option, telling him I would see him at dinner. I waved as he drove off, then went back inside the school, in time for math class. Hubert found me at lunch to check on my condition, offering another apology. I didn't have any hard feelings and reassured him of no future conflicts. The rest of the day went without any more incidents.

When I got home mom was waiting for me. I barely walked through the door before I was accosted by her probing fingers. She grabbed me and pulled my face close to hers, examining the stitching that wasn't present when I first left the house.

"Let go," I said pushing down her hands. "I'm fine, it was just a little cut," I said stepping back. "I'll live, you don't need to worry."

Mom smiled, "the waitress said you were in quite a state." "I just want to make sure my baby's alright," Mom said reaching back for my face.

"I'm fine, it was just an accident with a door," I said reassuringly, telling her how it happened.

"Well after dinner we will have to get those glasses adjusted," she said pointing to my crooked frames.

"Sounds good," I said escaping down the stairs to wait for my dad to get home from work.

Hiding in Plain Sight

Graduating into high school was a huge deal. The new school was massive. With over eight hundred grade ten students in attendance and over two thousand people inhabiting the building. The hallways were always cramped and busy. There was no time for any type of insubordination or disobedience in any of my classes. The teachers were focused on the lessons and didn't have time for any of my behavioral distractions. I thought it to be in my best interest to just melt into the crowd and not rock the boat. This wasn't the place for that.

I spent the next three years with my head down and my mouth shut. Doing my best to stay unnoticed and off the radar. The classes were full of students who were more than happy to ask questions about the lessons. I usually found the response to their questions satisfy any inquiry I might have had myself. I never raised my hand and only spoke up when it was absolutely necessary. I found out quickly that I could learn more by watching the mistakes of others and not making the same missteps of my own.

There were several occasions where I needed to step out from the sidelines, whenever a front of the class presentation was required, and I loathed those moments. Anxious to stand in the front of the room with all eyes on me. I didn't crave any sort of attention and when I got some, I just wanted to escape as quickly as possible. English class was the worst for the nerve-racking experiences, but I survived.

The required project was simple enough, I needed to debate a topic with another student, and the most compelling argument would get the better grade. I was still riding high from the epic journey of the grade nine bike trip and chose a topic within that mastered skill set.

The debatable topic was on the safety of wearing a bike helmet. I chose the negative side of the argument, and another student was arguing the safety benefits. I let them go first. I didn't have anything prepared. I decided to make up my side of the argument on the spot, using their argument to fuel my rebuttal. They had some valid points to help in avoidance of brain damage. Then it was my turn to speak. I faced into the classroom, my pulse pounding loudly in my ears, and started to speak.

"Bike helmets are a bad idea," I started my voice cracking as it broke through the silence. "Wearing a helmet gives the rider a false sense of security," taking a quick breath. "When a bike rider wears a helmet, they will be more reckless and try stunts and take risks that they shouldn't be taking."

Remembering to breath I finished off with, "any questions?"

I looked out into the room, thirty pairs of eyes looking back in my direction. I watched as a few hands raised into the air with questions about my twelve second presentation. (I still hold the record for shortest presentation ever.) I looked over the room, making eye contact with some of the students with raised arms.

"So, no questions then." I said with disregard for the raised hands. "Thank you," I said firmly and went back to my seat in the middle row of the classroom, as quickly as possible.

The class clapped a weak applause for the lackluster presentation. The teacher moved into the center of the blackboard at the front of the room, calling on the next two debaters. As the class waited for them to get ready for their presentations, the teacher referred to the length of time that the future presenters were required to achieve as they stood up at the front of the class. I did my part, not expecting a top grade, but I did a presentation none the less. I survived and that's all I needed to do.

The next month, once again in the English class we needed to do a show and tell type presentation in front of the class. I was still nervous and chose to do mine on how to change a flat tire on a bike. I had detached the wheel from my bike that morning, twisting the quick release handle to remove the rim from the front of the bike. The tire didn't fit in my locker, so it needed to be carried around to all the classes that I had that day. It was a royal pain, but I was confident in my abilities to change the innertube and give a good presentation, so it was mostly worth the hassle.

English class was my third period, my nerves was starting to wain the closer the time got to the presentation. I got to class and waited for my turn, sitting in my desk fidgeting before I was called on to present at the front of the room. I got up from my desk, taking the tire, and some tools that I had in my bag up to the front table. The teacher made a comment about my presentation needing to be longer than last months. I smiled at her and nodded understanding, not making any promises.

"Hello, today I will teach you how to change a flat tire on your bike." I said, half mumbled, with my eyes not lifting from the table.

"First you will need to remove all the air from the tire," I said as I uncrewed the cap off the innertubes stem, all my attention focused on the tire.

I pressed the stem of the valve and let the air squeak out of the inflated tube. Letting the airs removal eat up as many of the long seconds of the three-minute presentation as possible. My nervous finger accidently slid over the valve causing the escaping air to make a squealing fart sound on its way out of the shrinking inner tube. The class laughed at the flatulent sound. I looked up horrified that whole class thought I had tooted, seeing a reassuring thumbs up from a friend in the back row I continued less concerned about the silly sound.

Once all the air was removed, I went on to explain how to break the seal of the rubber tire from the rim. I used a screwdriver to pry in between the rubber tire and steel rim. Rotating the tool around the wheel opening a gap so that the innertube could be removed through the space. I pulled out the limp tube and placed it on the table.

"Now we need to locate the hole in the tube and patch it up." I said, focused on the patch kit I pulled from my bag.

I stretched out the tube, explaining that the holes were not always obvious and sometime a wet cloth was needed to find the exact spot with the hole. The puncture will bubble from the applied moisture, making the location of the hole easier to identify. My tube didn't have a hole, so I just gave the explanation and pulled out some patches from the kit. I showed how to apply the patch and then explained how to get the tube back onto the rim.

I showed how to reset the one side of the tire tread that was now outside the rim. Squeezing it back inside the steel rim to fully reassemble the tire. The final step was to check the valve stem. I explained that slobbering on a finger then slathering the spit onto the valve would make sure that no air was escaping. I finished up by reminding them to put the valve cap over the stem as another layer to keep the air inside the tire. I didn't bring a pump so they would just have to take my word for it. I finished the presentation with record precision and ninety seconds remaining on the clock.

"Thank you," I concluded "any questions," I said as I packed up my tool kit and prepared to rush back to my seat.

A single hand rose up from the right side of the class. It was one of the students I had ignored at the end of the last presentation. That moment from the last months presentation lingered with me, I wasn't happy about it. I needed to face my weakness and take the question.

"Yes, what is your question, please?" I asked pointing over in her direction.

"How did you learn how to change a bike tire so quickly?" she asked with a cute, dimpled smile.

I felt my cheeks glow warm before I answered, "well, I ride a lot and needed to become self reliant on changing a flat." "So, I have had some practice, hopefully making it look easy."

I went on to explain that I did all my own repairs from changing tire tubes to fixing the bikes chain when it snaps. I pulled out the multitool that adjusted all the bolts and explained how it could raise the bike seat or straighten out the handlebars. After my quick explanation the class applauded, signaling the completion of my presentation. I had almost managed to use the full three minutes, missing the mark by an eternity of twenty-two seconds. I went back to my desk, dreading that I had to carry the flat tire around with me for the rest of the day. I gave a sigh of relief and settled in to listen to the next presentation, happy that I was finished mine.

The rest of the high school classes were great if there were no presentations required. I managed to keep out of sight and out of trouble for the most part, managing to escape the hallways of grade ten mostly unscathed and unnoticed.

Making Art

Grade Eleven got more exciting, there were option classes this year, and they were the best part of the school's planned torment. Art class was always my favorite. Getting to paint or getting my hands dirty with clay were the most satisfying moments. Anything that got to stretch my imagination was exciting.

The art teacher was friendly and always quick to give advise on how to make the best art possible. She only had one rule, and I didn't find it very hard to follow. Absolutely no butterflies. She shared a story the year before of how she was terrified of the harmless creatures. Her phobia started when she almost fell off a mountain trail to her death in the avoidance of the colorful insect. So, she instituted the classroom as a butterfly free zone. She was lucky everyone loved her, and none of the students filled her art room with the winged bugs. Sharing your biggest fear with students was risky but it did guarantee no butterfly art.

The semesters art class project was to make a clay bowl that was unique and fancy. But before we could start with the clay, we needed to make our own tools. The following week was used to craft some clay carving tools. I pounded a heavy gauge wire with a hammer to flatten out one end, crafting it into a dull knife blade. The excess wire was wrapped up at the top, making a looping handle. Once the tools were complete, we were given our block of clay to sculpt into something that would be unique and special.

I found some amusement freaking out the girls that sat at the elevated table with me. I would wrap my index finger with a thin layer of clay, then run the dull blade of my newly crafted knife over the pad of my fingertip. The slice in the clay would look like a savage injury without any actual damage to the finger. The looks of shock and horror as I ran the blade over my finger turned to relief as I revealed the trick with a cheeky grin. The trick that I played not getting the response I was hoping for was quickly abandoned, and the project started.

I made my block of clay into a three-legged bowl with pointed hooks that protected the inner portion. When the wet clay was done being formed by my artistic hands, it was placed in the kiln and cooked into its permanent form. My monstrous bowl emerged from the extreme heat with an unplanned crack down the side. I didn't mind the addition; it gave the project some added character. When the clay was settled, layers of black and grey paint were added to the creation. The final project turned out well and has stood the test of time, residing on my dresser for the last twenty-five years.

The next semester I took a photography class and got to make a pin hole camera. The painted coffee can was only able to take a single picture, but I got to develop it myself under the red lights of the dark room. The picture came out blurry and unmemorable, but the process was enlightening.

Shop class was probably the most beneficial. We got to build a wall. It was three feet wide and six feet tall, it needed to be framed, setup for electricity, and be completely drywalled. Once the wall was finished, we would cut into the drywall and install a bathroom medicine cabinet. I remember all the drywall dust and the white stained teeth of the handsaw. Those were great days. That class was the most hands on, giving skills and insight into future home renovation projects.

Demolition Derby

In grade twelve I took a drivers education course for some extra credits. Over the previous summer I had got a job at the golf course down the street, making some **space for golf**. I saved up my minimum wage and just before graduation purchased my first car. It took a while, but I had managed to save the twelve hundred dollars required to obtain my first vehicle. It was a 1987 yellow Camaro. This car was awesome.

On the hot summer days the T-top roof could be removed, making the car feel like a convertible, the wind blowing over the windshield into the car. On the rainy days the removable roof panels leaked, the water would pour onto the front seats. I always kept a towel wedged in the sun visor to absorb most of the unwanted leakage, solving the problem for the most part. The hundred and thirty horsepower engine roared from under the hood. The rumble from the car would shake the street from a block away. This was not a stealthy vehicle.

It was a fun car to drive, the rear-wheel-drive horsepower was ready to squeal the tires at every set of traffic lights. The unstoppable urge to do donuts was rarely contained. I would spin the car in dust raising gravel every chance I could. When I worked at the golf course, I needed to make repairs to the equipment at the driving range. This would give me the opportunity to kickup dust clouds almost every week.

with the hatch back trunk and the back seats put down the car had a ton of space inside. It worked out great for helping my friends move out from their parents' homes to their first apartments. One occasion we even managed to squeeze a futon mattress in the back of the Camero, it stretched to fill up the entire compartment, but it fit none the less.

Those were the good old days, gas was cheep, and there wasn't a camera in every pocket. I would take the car out into the nearby neighborhoods, looking for new places to kick up dirt and spin the tires. I found a nearby baseball diamond that backed onto one of the main roads. I wanted to run the bases in my unnoticeable, bright yellow car. The field was blocked off from the street with a single wire fence, but I didn't let that stop me. I pushed the front end of the car slowly into the wire, the force of the newly applied tension slid the connecting brackets off the wire, and it fell to the ground with the loop disengaged. I drove onto the field and raced over to the ball diamond, excited to kick up a cloud of the red shale dust. After a few victory laps I took off, escaping the field through the gap I had created in the fence. Not wanting to give anyone enough time to call the police on my baseball diamond shenanigans.

It didn't take long before I found some new ways to cause trouble in my easily distinguishable yellow car. Using the alleyways of the nearby neighborhoods, a few of us would drive our cars into the steel garbage cans that lined the backstreets. The empty cans would dent easily as the tumbled loudly down the gravel roads. The laughter inside the car was loud and obnoxious.

It didn't take long for us to graduate into larger stationary objects to ram our vehicles into. Shopping carts were the most fun you could possibly ever have. Stalking up behind an abandoned cart, tapping into the steel frame and pushing it up to speed was a hilarious thrill. Once the cart had its speed up to around twenty plus kilometers an hour, I would ease the brakes of the car, letting the cart speed off ahead. The cart would hit the parking lot curb and would tumble and flip into the grass, catching some major air. We would all laugh hard, our cheeks and bellies burning at the stupidity. We were lucky that at this moment in time there were not cameras on every corner to catch our vehicular vandalism. I was smart enough to abandon such activities long before I was ever reported or captured by the shopping cart police.

The car that I drove was built strong and never caught any unwanted damage from the sundown shenanigans. I never needed to explain a random scratch or dent to my father who surely would have noticed any such addition to the car.

My friends and I all had our own cars, none of them were particularly fancy so we would mistreat them in ways that would be deemed unacceptable if they cost more than a thousand dollars.

We would play silly car games like follow the leader. This was essentially a chase, where you would drive around the streets and take the following vehicles on a scenic tour of the neighborhoods. On this occasion I was the driver of the second car, following behind the leader. The lead car pulled into the drive thru and ordered a chicken nugget snack from the first window.

I pulled up to the order window and told the lady taking orders, "nothing for me today, thanks."

She looked at me with confusion, her face not understanding why I would be in the drive thru line without wanting to order something.

I watched as the bag of food was being handed out of the takeout window and pushed my car into the bumper of the car in front of me. The car lurching forward; the bag still being held out the window by the worker. Her head leaning out the window to see what was going on.

The driver of the lead car telling her, "Hold on a second," putting their car into reverse and bumped back into me.

The workers eyes were giant sized as she watched a drive thru tractor pull. Our cars pushed against each other, engines growling in competition. After a few long moments the bag of fries and chicken lumps were collected and the lead car sped off.

I pulled up to the drive thru window and told the shocked burger employee, "nothing for me today, thanks!" Speeding off with a tire chirp, laughing so hard I could barely breathe.

That's another bad behavior interaction I'm happy there were no cameras available to capture. We might have scared that employee for life with our bumper car stupidity.

I drove that yellow car for a few short years, until the vehicles age made it more costly to repair the mechanical breakdowns then it was worth. I was tired of having the rain leak into the car, it always seemed to land in my lap, making it look like I had peed my pants.

The last straw was when I went to have a job interview at the computer store, being early I decided to get the car washed. I went through an automatic car wash and the water poured into the car. I should have known better, but my pants were soaked.

I was lucky that I had an hour until my interview and managed to be mostly dry by the time I went inside. I still had dirty crotch stains on my fresh khaki pants and needed to explain my messy condition. They must not have cared too much because I got the job.

The computer store was fun for awhile, giving me a new place to flex my distain for the rules and see how far I could push my luck.

Just Like Dracula

My father was fearless and when he was angry the ground would shake. So, when I saw fear in his eyes I approached with caution.

Dads favorite ten days of the year were that of the Calgary Stampede. He would rush home from work, change into his cowboy hat and old boots then drive our family down to the grounds. We would attend show every single day. Dad loved it.

Once the admission was paid, we would rush over to the first fiddlestick stand we could find. The ice-cream on a stick was his favorite. The vanilla ice-cream was covered with chocolate and nuts, giving it a variety of flavors. The first ice-cream of the season was always the best. But by the last day of stampede, we had our fill and didn't want to see a fiddlestick for the rest of the year. Dad would devour his cold treat in seconds, immediately looking for the next stampede snack to devour. The nuts from the ice-cream and would always get stuck under his false teeth. As my father searched the grounds, he would spit out the tiny, dislodged chucks of half chewed peanuts. It was disgusting, but this was the Stampede, and he fit right in.

We walked under the gondola that ran the length of the grounds. Its elevated cable transporting people from one end of the lot to the other. We all laughed as we reminisced of how my cowboy boot fell off years before. The cowboy boots were two sizes too big, and I wore them year-round, they were my favorite. We went for the scenic ride as a family, filling up the bench seat. My legs kicking as they dangled off the seat, the left boot fell from my small foot. I felt the boot slip off and fall. I looked over the safety bar just in time to see it strike an unsuspecting man in the head. The cables continued to pull the seats to the far end of the grounds, and we laughed at the surprise the man must have had when my size six shitkicker fell from the sky. We reached the end of the line, disembarked the ride to quickly, planning to return to the spot where the boot had dropped off. We found the man standing with the boot in his hand. He was in good spirits about the ariel assault, and we all had a good chuckle. The man was quick to forgive the transgression and gave my boot back. We all laughed as Dad retold the story.

We found our way into the basement of the big four building. The bottom level was filled with people looking for delicious meals. This area was transformed into a communal picnic area with hundreds of tables to share with all the other guests. The wooden tabletops were covered with a red and white cowboy plaid tablecloth. We found a space to sit that would accommodate our four seats. My sister and I gave Dad our requested orders. The food court was transformed into a multicultural tapestry of culinary delights, but all we wanted was a slice of greasy pizza.

My sister and I sat and waited patiently for his return. We would watch all the people go by with their delicious looking meals. The smell of the food court was intoxicating, it was a great place to escape the smell of the cows, and their stink that lingered over the grounds. Dad would return quickly with our deliciously soggy pizza and some sodas, then venture back out to get my mother and his chosen dinners. He would always come back with some sausages and perogies, those were his favorite, and mom didn't mind them either. After a quick meal we would clean up our space at the picnic table then return outside to the sunshine in search of more ice-cream.

Historically the week of stampede is hot, but Calgary being one of those "if you don't like the weather, wait five minutes," type of cities, the clouds had rolled in threatening a storm while we were inside. Dad had the whole week planned out based on snacks, so a bit of rain was not going to slow him down any. We would use this time to go check out the exhibition hall and avoid the soon arriving rainfall.

We walked our way into the largest building on the grounds and pulled open the doors just as the heavens opened. The large rain drops cooled down the pavement instantly. A thunderous rumble could be heard off in the distance shaking inside the clouds. This was a great time to be inside.

We weren't even five steps inside the doors, and you could smell it. That sweet smell of cinnamon could only mean one thing, mini doughnuts. We were barely able to keep up to Dad as he raced over to watch the doughnuts fall off the conveyor into the sugar below. Dad ordered a large bucket for us all to share and we watched through the glass as each one of the sugared treats moved from the boiling oil into the sugar. The first doughnuts out of the bucket were always too hot for consumption, but we all took the chance, and devoured the fresh cinnamon covered doughnuts. The bucket quickly emptied as Dad offered out the last one a few minutes later.

Once the treats were gone, we would all disburse slightly. Lisa would stay with my mom, and I would wander away with my dad. The exhibition building was filled with all sorts of things to see. There were people doing live infomercials, showing the growing crowds how the product, they were trying to sell worked. People would stand around and watch the presentations before making their purchasing decisions.

Dad was always interested in the formula that kept his boots shined up to perfection, so we wandered off in that direction. He bought a new bottle of the boot elixir every year, its secret formula working wonders. Dad never passed up the opportunity for the lady to show him how wonderful it worked. He would raise his boot up to the elevated platform, and have the boot polished. Once the boot was buffed, we would ask if the other could be done, if he purchased a bottle, of course. That was always the hook, the salesperson would only tidy up the one boot, leaving the other boot looking sad and dirty. With the prospect of a guaranteed sale the lady cleaned the second boot.

Dad purchased his already planned bottle of boot cleaner, and we continued checking out all the other vendors, looking for the next treasure for the or treat for our bellies.

Dad and I progressed down the row of vendors and approached a group of people watching a man using an amazingly absorbent mop. This was one of the corner vendors and they had a bunch of chairs setup, so people could be comfortable while watching the sales performance. Dad sat down to take a rest and get something out of his false teeth.

"Wait here," I told him "I'm going to go find mom, and Lisa," I said. "We will meet you back here in a few minutes."

He nodded as he fished the bottom plate out of his mouth, looking for the cause of his discomfort. It was disgusting and I hurried away before seeing what he would find.

I found my mom and sister a few stalls back looking at transparent toilet seats. My sister was trying to convince my mother to get the one with goldfish suspended in the clear resin, but she had no luck.

"Dads over at the corner, with the mops," I told them. "And we are going to meet him at the seats over there, before going into the art exhibit that's in the next room over."

The prospect of seeing all the fancy indigenous art helped to hurry them along. We returned to the seat a few minutes later, the show was over, and Dad was gone.

We decided that he must have gone into the art exhibit without us and followed in after him. We went into the large room that was filled with stampede themed statues and paintings. The art was a modern depiction of cowboys and Indians and was fascinating to see. The craftmanship of each piece of art was breathtaking. The room was dimly lit with spotlights aimed at the art; it took a moment for my eyes to adjust. As my eyes focused, I could see my dad deeper inside the room.

I left my mom and sister, looking at a rodeo statue, and rushed over to my father. They could take their time looking at all the art pieces that pulled at their interest. As I approached my dad, I noticed that something wasn't quite right. He was frozen in place, mid step, like one of the statues, not moving a single muscle. His back was to me, so I greeted him as I approached.

"What are you doing?" I asked him as my father was not one to just stand there looking silly

His arms were raised up in a karate stance, and he was not moving, frozen stiff like a bronze statue.

"Are you trying to be a piece of art?" I asked confused.

"Did you see him?" Dad asked with concern.

"No, who?" I asked.

"You know, him, is he gone?" Dad said doubling down.

"No, I just see you standing here like a statue, being weird." I said, moving around to look at him directly.

As I got in front of him, I could see fear in my fathers' eyes. He wasn't being a statue for fun, he was frozen stiff from fear. Just then Down Syndrome Pete walked by and growled in Dad's general direction. A fresh jolt of fear flicked across his eyes, and his body twitched, fighting the urge to run away.

"Him!!!" Dad said not moving his mouth when he talked.

Then Down Syndrome Pete returned intrigued by this strange man standing like a statue, wearing a cowboy hat, shiny boots and raised karate chop arms. Pete gave another growl and moved along, not interested in whatever my dad was doing.

"What's wrong with you?" I asked with more wonder than concern.

"Is he gone?" Dad said, still not moving his lips.

I looked over in the direction that Pete had moved and confirmed his departure from the art exhibit. I took hold of Dads' arm, and his body relaxed enough for him to drop the karate stance.

"what's wrong with you?" I asked again, now with just wonder.

"You seen him, right?" "He tried to make me one of them." Dad said looking around to make sure Pete had actually left.

"Make you one of them? what? I asked not knowing where this was going.

"You know, retarded." He said in a whisper as if saying the word would somehow summon the kid back.

"What." I said, "how do you figure that?"

"Well, if they bite you, you turn retarded, you know like Dracula." Dad explained "that's how they multiply."

"That's not down syndrome kids, that's vampires, the ones that sparkle in the sunlight." I laughed at his absurd explanation. "Let's go find mom." I said, pulling on his arm.

"Yea, lets get out of here, before they return to get me." He agreed, looking around for the ambush.

I laughed at his absurd reaction. "Yea, they want you really bad." "You could be their king." I teased.

"Don't say that." Dad said as he continued to look around.

We found my mom and sister and left the art exhibit, impressed by the years entries. Just as we were about to get into the main room, I grabbed Dad and let out a growl. He took off in a high step run, his knees almost clipping his chin. We all laughed at his funny walk. After about ten feet he stopped and turned around, telling us we weren't being funny.

We made it back outside and the storm had already come and gone. The clouds had parted, and the sun had returned to dry up the quickly shrinking puddles. We were off to find our next unique treat, or another of the fiddlesticks. We had some time until Dads next scheduled event was to take place.

One of our favorite activities at the stampede is to enjoy the shows on the outdoor stage. The live music was a fantastic way to spend the late afternoons, sitting on the grass, drinking soda and eating hotdogs. Dad wasn't fond of many of the new bands that were featured that year, but one had caught his attention. Paul Revere and the Raiders. They were going to preform, and he planned to be in attendance. They were going to sing one of his favorite songs, Louie; Louie, and he was going to be there to see it. We waited patiently for the show to begin, eating our fifth round of snacks.

The sun had started to set, and the band finally took to the stage. We had waited over an hour for this moment. Dad lost his mind when the band walked out. He hooted and hollered as they played his favorite songs. After a few lesser-known songs, the band got down to business and played the much-anticipated Louie Louie. Dad loved every minute of it and absorbed every single second. Once the song was over, he was ready to go home, completely satisfied. It had been a long day, and we were coming back tomorrow, and the next day, until the ten days were over.

We made it back to the car just in time to see the fireworks launch into the sky, signifying the end of the grandstand show. I was asleep before we got home, dreaming of tomorrows stampede adventure.

If Looks Could Kill

Every year our family's favorite stage show at the stampede was the hypnotist. It was a different show every time we got to see it. You never knew how the volunteers would react to the suggestions. The show had the same rhythm every time and we had seen it enough to be almost able to recite the hypnotist's script. The way he ran the show was the only thing that was structured, everything else was left up to chance and the way the volunteers subconscious interpreted the suggested commands.

Terry the Hypnotist stated the show the same way every time, by asking for volunteers from the audience. He would pick out a dozen willing participants and have them go up on stage. The already laid-out chairs would quickly fill with people who were willing to be part of the show. He would then try and place them into a state of extreme relaxation. Talking slowly and with purpose, he would put them to sleep. Some people were more open to the suggestions than others, falling quickly under his spell. The participants that fought against the charm and didn't respond to the suggestions were removed from the stage and returned into the crowd. Once he had the selected cast for the show, he would begin putting them deeper into his trance.

He would tell them that they are sleepy and that their arms were light as a single feather. If the tranced cast responded, their arms would start to float into the air. The deeper they were under his spell the higher their arms would raise. The people on the stage were deep within his grips, and so was the lady sitting directly in front of me. Her arms were outstretched towards the sky, and her head was slumped forward. Once Terry turned his attention from the cast back to the audience sitting on the grass, he noticed the not so rare, hypnotized spectator. He made a quick joke and asked for her name.

Her boyfriend quickly shouted out "Sara"

Terry paced the stage thinking of a cheeky suggestion to give to Sara.

"Sara, when is snap my fingers you will awake, but every time I touch my nose the person behind you will grab your ass." Terry finished the suggestion and snapped his fingers.

The crowd's attention all turned to look at Sara. There gaze looking past her, towards me, sitting directly behind her. Terry reached up and scratched her nose. Sara reacted, but didn't move much. Terry reached up for a second scratch. Now Sara was frustrated, a single touch could have been excused as an unintentional contact but twice was unacceptable. She leaned over to whisper something to her boyfriend of the transgression. The crowd chuckled. Terry reached up for a third scratch, and she snapped.

"Stop!" she yelled at me "or my boyfriend is going to kick your ass." She threatened with fire in her eyes.

The boyfriend looked over at me and shrugged his shoulders. He was in on the joke but still needed to stand up for his woman.

Terry took this moment to adjust the situation.

"Sara, are you all right out there, would you be more comfortable up here on stage with us?" "Come on up." He instructed.

She looked around confused that Terry knew her name but stood up and approached the stage anyway. Once on her feet and a few steps away, she looked back in my direction, and if looks could kill. She pointed two fingers at her eyes then back to me, the international sign for "I got my eye on you." The crowd laughed at her hand signals and cheered as she approached closer to the stage.

Once she was standing next to Terry he asked, "what's going on out there?" "You looked uncomfortable."

"Yea, some little perve was grabbing my ass!" Sara explained, pointing out to my general direction as the crowd laughed.

Terry reached up and scratched his nose and Sara jumped, looking confused as I grabbed at her from over fifty feet away.

"He's still doing it." She said, still processing the imaginary sticky fingers. Looking back over her shoulder.

"All the way from over there?" Terry asked, pointing out into the crowd. "How do you think he is doing it?" he enquired.

"I don't know," Sara said angrily. "But I don't like it, and my boyfriend is going to kick his ass!" the crowed roared with laughter at the empty threat.

"Go grab a seat," Terry instructed her to one of the empty chairs on stage, "I'll have a word with all the perverts in the audience." He said with a chuckle and a grin.

Once Sara was in her stage chair, Terry approached her and tapped her gently on the forehead, she fell into the deep sleep immediately. He removed the suggestion of his itchy nose and got me off the hook. The boyfriend looked over to me and assured me that I was in no danger, and that he knew it was a hypnosis trick. I gave a small wave in acceptance of the acknowledgement and turned my attention back to enjoy the rest of the show.

The cast put on a great show, making the crowd laugh at their ridiculous antics from the standard list of hypnotic suggestions. At the conclusion of the show the crowd roared and clapped for all the hypnosis participants as they returned to their seats in the grass. Sara retuning to her boyfriends' side showing me one more death stare, squinting out an angry gaze that was full of bad intentions.

Terrys final suggestion always was for the participants to call into the stampede and request his return the following year. And they must call in, because we return to watch the hypnosis show every year. It's the best part of the stampede, every show is the same, but every show is unique. But that one time, I was accused of playing some grab ass, was the closest I ever got to being involved in the show.

Don't You Know Who I Am?

One day at college I made mention that I was looking for a job while sitting around the lunch table at Mount Royal. One of Mikes classmates was the manager of a computer store and told me I should stop in for an interview and get a job working with him. I told him that I would be there, as having his personal recommendation would almost guarantee me a quick chance at employment.

I drove across town to the store and arrived way to early. Ten minutes is fine but an hour, that was too much. I decided a quick carwash would burn up some of the time and went over to the gas station to clean up the car. I should have known better, the moment the carwash started dirty water poured into my car. The defective sealing mechanism on the T-tops barely kept out the rain, so a pressurised bust of water showered in unhindered. My khaki pants were soaked, marked with the dirty water that rained inside the car. I had a towel in the back seat that I used to dry off as best I could, but the pants were still stained. It would take an hour to get home to change and

I didn't have that much time, and missing the interview was not an option. So, I went in with mostly dry pants, and a excuse ready if they noticed.

I went into the store and was directed to the front office. I opened a nondescript door and went inside. It was a cozy room, with a couple of desks and a sofa. I met with the lady in charge, and she offered me the job without much of an interrogation.

"Alan says your good, so if you want the job, it's yours." She said with a smile.

"Yes, I would, when can I start?" I asked eager to have new employment.

The golf season was ending in a few weeks, and my weekend work was going to be over. I mentioned of my other commitments and was told I could work the evenings and weekends. This was going to be perfect. I was hired on as one of the cashiers. I was given a green shirt and told that I could start the following evening. I thanked her for the opportunity and quickly left before she could ask more questions.

I arrived early for my first shift the next day. The drive over to the store was easy, the leaves had just begun to turn, their bright colors would soon fall from the trees. I made it to the store before the sun started to set. I didn't have to drive into the brightness of the setting sun, the days were getting shorter and soon it would be dark midafternoon.

I went into the font office and was introduced to the other cashier for the evening who was going to train me. I was anxious to be a cashier. I was nervous about making mistakes with the money.

"Ah, your Alans friend," Katie greeted with a cute smile. "I will have you trained up in no time."

"Thank you, can't wait." I said following her over to the registers.

The tills were setup back-to-back. We both worked inside a boxed space with the two outside counters dividing us from the customers. Our computer monitors and cash drawers were next to each other with no divider. Katie walked me through the process for the first few customer transactions, then I was on my own.

I took to the program quickly and soon knew all the required functions. If I had any questions, she was right over my shoulder to be asked. As the night went on the other staff wandered past to introduce themselves. Most of them made mention that I was Alans friend and asked how we knew each other. I told them that we went to school together, not offering much more than that. I quickly realized that they all thought he and I were best friends and were trying to score some favor. I didn't correct the assumption and used the misunderstanding to my advantage.

Most of my shifts were on the weekend after my day had finished at the golf course. I would just have enough time to get home, change into my deep green computer shirt, then drive to the store across town before the shift started. When I arrived at the store, I would be hungry from a hard day of riding mowers and warring with the marshals. I would sign in at the front of the store, then ask Katie if she wanted to go get some dinner. There was always a second cashier working, so the station was never unattended on our departure.

We would step out and grab some chicken nuggets or a sandwich, returning within less than an hour. We would go out for dinner most of the shifts that we worked together. She was questioned about the excursions only once, no one ever asked me about it. She told them that it was my idea, and that was the end of it. We continued to go out for our dinners. No one wanted to upset Alan over the time I took away from the store and never bothered to bring it up. The false assumption that we were best friends kept me insulated from any repercussions. The fact was that we only had lunch at school, sitting at the same table on occasion. We didn't even have any classes together. I barely knew Alan at all, but that was my secret to keep.

After a while Katie found a better job where her skills would truly be valued, and she left the store for that opportunity. Her position was quickly filled with a younger kid that knew one of the other managers.

Jake was funny and felt that he had the same level of insulation that I had. He probably had more just by actually knowing the person that got him the job.

Jake and I worked at the front counter together for a few weeks. The customers would split the line, choosing between the two if us for their purchase transactions. It was a busy Saturday; the line of customers was starting to get longer, as everyone tried to leave the store at the same time. I was working on the customers order on my side of the cash station, when I heard Jake getting some flack from the lady on his side of the counter. I could overhear her complaint, something of the excessive amount of time she had spent in line waiting to pay. I felt a pull on my shoulder and half turned around to look at Jake.

"What a bitch," he said loudly with a clear tone, then returned his attention back to her transaction as if nothing had just happened.

I didn't even have a moment to respond. The customer at my counter was laughing hard, as I gave him a shrug. I was scared to look over directly and only peeked over my shoulder to see Jakes customer, her jaw agape, totally flabbergasted at what had just happened. She was holding cash in her hand and Jake pulled it from her fingers, finishing the transaction, handing back some change and the receipt.

"Have a nice day." He said as she turned to leave.

Her mouth still open, not having the words to express herself. Once she was out the door, we both lost it. My customer lingered and we all had a good laugh. Wiping a tear from my watering eyes I welcomed the next customer who didn't dare make a complaint of having to wait in line, knowing we were all sold out of fucks to give.

I stayed as a cashier for a few more months, watching from the perch at the front of the store as it degraded into all out chaos. The salesmen started to physically fight over customers, smacking each other in the nuts, then chasing each other around the stores like maniacs. It was beginning to become an embarrassment to be associated with that place. I made mention that I was thinking of leaving and was given a raise and a promotion. Anything to keep Alan's best friend happy.

Check the Cord

I was given a new job in the computer stores repair department. It would be my job to sign in the computers, getting the customers basic diagnostics as to what the machines problems were, then take the payments after the job was finished. It was cashier adjacent, but I didn't have to deal with every single customer, just those looking for repairs.

I got good at making over the phone computer diagnoses. It was funny how many times you would ask the person on the other end of the phone if the computer was plugged in, and how many times they would say no. It was the first question I asked every time, and it probably solved twenty percent of the problems.

Whenever a customer would bring in their machine, I would plug it in on the counter just to make sure it powered on. On more than one occasion a customer brought in their desktop computers complaining of a stuck disc drive. I would plug in the machine and with a single index finger, extended in the most pompous way possible, press the eject button. The drive would normally just automatically open. I would get a frustrated glare from the customer, mad that the drive didn't work at home. I would make the same lame joke every time about the computer wanting to see the rest of its family back at the store. No one ever laughed.

There were never any charges for this type quick of service, and my bad jokes were always free. If the disk drive still wouldn't open, I would pull out my already unfolded paper clip. I had one that was extended out of shape and would push it into the tiny manual release hole found on the front of every disc drive. Most people didn't even know the button was there. With some firm pressure, the drive door would creep open, just enough to get a fingertip grip. Pulling the tray out normally revealed a stack of discs jammed inside. I would make another terrible joke and return their equipment with the problem solved.

I encountered a vast array of people working at the counter and could spot a mac user from across the room. The smell and crazy Doc Brown hair were a dead giveaway. Mac users were a special breed. Most people didn't like to leave their machines for the week that it would normally take to get repaired.

One of my favorite customer interactions was with a sweet old lady that signed in her machine for repair, and when told it would take a few days to get diagnosed and fixed, she told me that she would wait. I watched as she wandered off and found a chair, posting up next to the service door and started to eat her lunch. I was impressed at her willingness to wait, coming prepared for a stay. I was worried that she might have planned to sleep over in the store overnight and pushed her machine to the front of the repair line. I told the repair staff of her aggressively polite tactic, and they peaked out the window to see her reading a book. They laughed and started on the computer virus removal from her machine immediately. Within an hour her machine was up and running, ready to go. I placed the tuned-up pc on the counter and called her over. I was greeted with a big grin.

"I knew you could do it!" she said with a cheeky wink.

I laughed and took her payment for the repair.

I was happy the repair team was able to move the mountains required for her not to take up a permanent residence in the store. Normally they were too busy screwing around to get any work done. They were good at the job and were able to fix a whole day's worth of machines in only a few hours, but that's all they would do.

The rest of the time they would act out scenes from their favorite movie "The Rock." This Nic Cage classic had a scene where he had to inject himself with the antidote to a toxic gas. Anytime a customer investigated the window to see the progress of the repairs they would put on a show. Dave would grab a giant syringe that was filled with a bright green cleaning fluid, fall to the floor and pretend to be convulsing in pain. He would then pretend to stab himself in the heart and administer the antidote. His recreation was flawless but never got the response he wanted from the customers, or maybe it did.

Normally the customer would rush away horrified at the production they had just unwillingly witnessed. If the unwanted attention from the customer stayed any longer, Dave would give them a pig nose on the window. He would stretch out his nostrils wide enough on the glass that you could see into his brain. On a full day shift I would watch this scene playout dozens of times, every time it happened it was funnier. Each customer had a different reaction, but none of them were happy with the pig nose or the brain inspection.

Future Home of Strippers

I worked at the service counter for a few months. I was learning lots of computer repair tricks every week. I even got to learn how to make some of the repairs.

Then I started to have problems with the schedules not being finished on time at the end of the week. When I went home from my Sunday shift, I never knew when I was supposed to return. Email wasn't a thing yet, so I had no way to know when I was supposed to work until they phoned the house to see why I wasn't at the store. It took an hour to drive to the store. I wasn't making a special trip, just to find the weeks unfinished schedule. So, I would wait for the calls. Sometimes I would already have planned to go to the movies with Erin and would tell them I wasn't available and not coming in. After awhile they just stopped calling altogether.

On a cool November morning I went to the mailbox to check for birthday cards, I didn't have any, but I did find my record of employment. I had been quietly terminated from my post at the computer store and wasn't very upset about it. I walked home from the mailbox, dreaming of the future free of the store.

I walked into the house and was informed by my mother that I had a call waiting. I answered the phone, and it was the store. I told them that I had just gotten their letter. Then I was asked if I wanted to come back and work at the store across from Chinook mall. I paused for a second as they tried to sell me on the idea. It was way closer to the house, I would get a raise, but I would be back at the cashier station. I agreed, only if the schedules would be out consistently. I was given this guarantee and asked to start the next evening. I agreed and hung up the phone, surprised by the coincidental interaction, but happy about the new opportunity.

I returned to the store the next night. The building was shaped like a giant cylinder, I was excited to see all the behind-the-scenes office spaces. The customer floor with the computer displays only made-up half of the buildings public area. I met with the store manager, and he took me around to meet the other sales staff. I was still being introduced as Alan's friend and that my role was to be team lead for the cashiers. I was going to be bullet proof. I would work at the tills, training the other cashiers all the tips and tricks to work arounds the cumbersome POS (point of sale, although it could also be considered the other acronym also) system. I was the only one in the building that knew how to process a customer return and chose to keep some of the finer tips and tricks to myself. It was nice to be needed.

It was almost Christmas, and the store was starting to get busy with the holiday rush. Management had brought some of the other stores sales team to help with the increased customer traffic. Being across the street from the cities busiest mall helped bring in all types of new computer customers. This store was twice as busy as the other location.

The two groups of salesmen didn't mix well and failed quickly, it was like oil and water. The two stores had different expectations for there staff and the ones from across town didn't like the changes to the pay structure. The bickering over commissions was brutal. Before long the pushing and shouting started again. I stayed working as a cashier until after the Christmas rush, then quit officially. In those final weeks I felt embarrassed to be associated with the store and couldn't escape it quick enough.

The computer store closed soon after, only staying open for a year after I had left. The reputation of the salesmen caused the customers to flee, not wanting the hassle of dealing with the unpredictability of an unhinged associate. Once the computer store moved out, the space was leased out for some other retail opportunities. They never seemed to be successful and moved out rather quickly from the odd shaped building. The building still stands in the same place today, I think it has been turned into a strip club. Its funny to think back on my time at the store, never knowing that one day it would be the future home of strippers but that's how the world turns.

The Next Adventure Was Super

Roger got me a job working with him at the grocery store. We had gone to both junior high and high school together and both did our best to not find much success at college. He told me of the job and all the fun that I was missing out on, and I was immediately interested. So, I went in to apply for the job. I talked with the department supervisor as Roger filled out my paperwork. I got paid after two weeks so he must have done an alright job. Getting to work with Roger in the housewares department was fantastic. It was like hanging out with a group of friends and getting paid to fool around. It didn't take long before management had us separated and put on different schedules, except for special assignments.

One of the reoccurring department events each year was the two months where the store tried to sell furniture. This was a grocery store after all so of course the customers would want to purchase new bedroom furniture every year. There was a bird flu epidemic that year and the company's purchasers couldn't travel to China to see all the furniture samples, so all the samples were sent to our store. Over a hundred unassembled boxes arrived and were put upstairs, above the barber shop and bank, in the dark and dusty storage space that existed up there. Roger and I were given the task of building all the random furniture pieces, so that the buyers could make their selections on what the store would sell the next furniture season.

The room was long and narrow, it had windows on both sides. One set looked out into the store providing the perfect vantage point for loss prevention to spy down on the customers, watching for shoplifters to stuff candy into their pockets. The other set of windows looked out into the parking lot, and they provided most of the light into the room. There were only a couple of weak lightbulbs that broke the lingering darkness. It was hot and dusty up there, but we were away from the public, so it was almost like a paid vacation.

Roger and I were given two weeks to build the hundred unmarked pieces of furniture. Each box was a mystery, it could be a table, a chair, or even a dresser. All the instructions were in Chinese, so we got good at building furniture without the use of instructions. This was not like Ikea furniture; the designs were not very intuitive. We had lots of pieces left over from every finished project. By the time our two-week deadline arrived, we had already been finished for two days.

We setup the dark room with dressers, end tables and headboards. Kitchen tables, twelve different styles of chairs, kitchen carts and a wine rack. The built furniture filled up the probably mouse infested space. When the hundred pieces of furniture were spread out you could barely move through the dingy space.

Roger and I were proud of our accomplishment and still don't need to look at instructions when building furniture.

Shortly after that furniture building adventure Roger went back to school to finish his university education. I never went back to school, but sometimes we would still work the rare weekend shift together.

I had quit my post secondary school adventure, finding my time at mount royal to be only filled with strawberry Sunday ice-cream and Hawaiian pizza. The classes were taught by people that didn't inspire a productive future, so I chose to not go back, focusing on work instead.

By not going back to class my work availability opened, and I was quickly given more hours at the store. I was soon promoted to the assistant of the assistant in the housewares department. I was going places.

After another year I was promoted all the way to department supervisor. I got to wear I tie every day and directed a team of ten dedicated slackers, that I fondly referred to as my kids. Some of them were old enough to be my parents, but they were my kids none the less. I called the regular customers my fans and that would make the kids laugh.

We had a good time curing cancer; I mean putting toasters on the shelves. Management would like to think our task was that vital, but we were just a grocery store after all.

You're Fired!

I never had to fire anyone and I'm happy about that. I was almost forced to, but the store manager was literally one step faster than I was that day.

He raised his chubby Italian finger to the sky and shouted, "your fired!"

I thought it was hilarious.

We were having trouble with that employee for a few weeks and his missed overnight shift was the last straw. I was forced to have a union meeting with him the week before about his missed shift and he was finally out of chances.

The union representative looked at me with skeptical eyes as we waited for Brett to arrive for his disciplinary meeting. Brett was always late and if I wanted to get any type of solution resolved I needed to involve the union. We watched the clock tick past Brett's scheduled start time. Twelve hundred seconds disappeared, until twenty minutes later, Brett walked up the stairs into the supervisor bullpen. The union rep was pissed and pulled Brett into the unoccupied managers office to have a private conversation. The union rep. was embarrassed at having to stand up for the late employee, expecting my claims to be fruitless. They only stayed in the room for a few moments before Brett walked out with his head held low, after the savage tongue lashing. I couldn't hear the conversation threw the door, but the muffled hiss vibrated the walls.

"Write him up for being late," the union man said firmly, "and when he is late again you can fire him." He looked over at Brett shooting daggers with his eye as he left.

I wrote out the paperwork and was given a promise from Brett of improvement. I took this chance to see if he was willing to work some night shifts with me. I was needing to work on a store renovation and needed some help. The back wall of the department was being removed, and the store was being stretched out another thirty feet into the parking lot and I needed some manpower. He was a thick kid and looked strong, that would be handy in the moving some of heavy things. Brett agreed and we planned to start the midnight shifts in a few days.

Brett showed up for the first night but not for the second. And that was the last straw. He wandered into the store at nine a.m. just as we were all ready to go home. The store manager, who had also worked all night, saw him out the corner of his eye, the same moment I did. We both rushed over towards Brett with bad intentions. The manager waving around his sausage fingers fired him on the spot. I was angry about the broken promise and didn't disagree with the termination solution. Brett walked out of the store with his head hung low, defeated by his inability to be on time.

Only Once

I had to go on the night shift on more than one occasion. The complete upheaval of my schedule played havoc on my mind. It was easy to stay up late and work through the night. The problem was when you needed to transition back to days, it would take weeks before your body adapted back to a normal person's schedule.

It was on the third night of working the graveyard shift, that's when I would start to see things, strange things, out of the corner of my eye. I swear one time a saw a leprechaun sitting in the put away bin. The bin was normally full of customer discarded items that needed to be put back on the shelf. I had walked past the bin a dozen times over that evening shift, and it was empty. The kids had done a good job before the sun went down and had managed to clean out the bin. With only a few hours until sunrise I walked into the back room, pushing the swinging doors open with the front of the squeaky wheeled pushcart.

As I walked into the stock room I could see a leprechaun siting in the bin. He was hunched over, barely fitting in the bottom of the stacked bins. I blinked a few times, trying to adjust my eyes to the darkened back room. After about five long blinks he finally disappeared with a wave and a cheeky smile. I stood in front of the doors until they stopped swinging, trying to make sense of what I had just seen. I walked forward slowly to inspect the bin and just as before it was still empty. Even if it wasn't and the leprechaun had left a gold coin, I knew better than to take it. Never trust a leprechaun.

I still had a few night shifts left, and I was already losing my mind. I was exhausted and could hardly wait to get home for some much-needed sleep.

I had been in the store since ten o'clock the night before, my shift ended at seven in the morning, and I was ready to go home. I stood patiently by the exit waiting for the clock to signify my scheduled departure. With only a few seconds left the door opened, and the store manager marched in, looking surprised that I was already going home.

"Oh, hey can you wait around a minute," he asked, "I want to check your progress and go over a couple of things."

"Sure, I can stay for a few minutes." I said reluctantly. My legs were tired, and I was ready to fall over.

"Good, I'll meet you in the department in five." He said, walking up the stairs to discard his jacket.

I wandered back to the housewares department and wandered the isles as I waited. If I stopped moving, I feared that my body would fall over, so like a shark I just kept moving to survive. Time went slowly and the five minutes took forever. Then the five minutes, turned into ten, then twenty. I was tired of waiting and went upstairs to check on the managers delay.

This asshole was eating jelly covered toast and reading the news paper. I walked up and gave a WTF shrug, squinting my eyes with disdain.

"Oh, I didn't forget about you, I'll be right down." He explained, knowing I wasn't impressed, but indicating he had a renewed sense of urgency.

I didn't say anything as I went back downstairs to my department, seething at his disrespect for wasting my time. I waited and waited. My kids started to come in for the morning shift at eight and were surprised to still see me there. I got a wave of rejuvenation as I stood with the kids and talked about how the survived the last few day shifts. Seventy-seven minutes had passed before the manager walked into my department. The kids scattered into their morning tasks as he approached.

"Ready for an inspection?" he asked.

"I was ready an hour ago?" I said with venom in my voice and contempt in my eyes.

"Great, lets go have a look at what was done last night." He said, understanding my displeasure, and not caring.

Store managers were always on a power trip, trying to interject the negative energy of their life into the rest of the staff. It was the standard "when I say jump" mentality, the I'm in charge and you will do whatever I say. Well, I don't jump for anyone, and certainly didn't treat my kids that way. I was taught to be a "follow me" type of leader from my fallen mentor Lee, so that's how I behaved.

We walked the isles and after we cleared the zone, I got my much-delayed feedback.

"Looks good." He said then scurred away like the rat he was, not waiting for the explosive rebuttal I was too tired to give.

I waived at the kids as I departed from the store, not wanting to waist another minute of daylight with my eyes open. I made it home and fell asleep instantly, knowing I had another shift at sundown.

I finished off another night shift without any issues and waited by the exit for the clock to digitally reach seven. The manager arrived again just as the clock struck. He was surprised to see me at the door ready to go.

"Oh hey, we need to do another walk through," he said with his coffee cup sloshing with his movements.

"Sounds good," I said with a big smile. "I'll meet you over there in five." I said, walking out the door towards my car, with no intention of coming back for the inspection.

I'm not falling for that twice. I went home and had the best sleep, dreaming of past adventures, until my alarm woke me for the last night shift of the cycle.

The night shift went by quickly, I was excited to have a couple of days off to rejoin the land of the living. At the end of the shift, I was ready and waiting to go, standing by the door at seven. The manager walked in right on schedule.

"Oh hey, I looked for you yesterday." He said waiting for an excuse.

"I was there, you must not have looked hard enough." I said with a big smile. We both knew I was long gone.

"Well, we need a walk through today." He said, not happy about my blatant disobedience.

"Sure, you have five minutes, lets go through it right now," I said turning towards the department. "Its now or never."

The look of shock on his face was priceless. No one dared stand up for themselves. I shattered his illusion of power and control. He stood stunned for a few seconds then followed me down the main isle to the housewares department.

We walked the isles in silence and when we finished the last row, he squeaked out a weak "looks good."

"Of course it does," was my only response in a sarcastic tone.

We walked back down the main isle. I picked up the pace and got to the exit door a few steps ahead of him. I went out the door and he went up to the office to have a good cry. I was satisfied with the interaction and didn't give him a chance to impose his false bravado on me. The manager never tried to ever again anyway, knowing I was impervious to his non-existent authority.

I slept through most of the next two days to rejuvenate, excited to be back at work in the daytime, excited to see the kids and my fans.

Under New Management

A short while later I was transferred to another store. It was closer to my house, and I was ready for the new challenge. I was given a different department and joined home and garden. This was a great department; it changed with the seasons, and I would be outside for the summer in the garden center. But being dropped into an already established department meant that I inherited the last supervisors' kids and all their bad habits.

I was determined to get them working how I wanted them too, with my standard tactics of being a follow me type of leader. Whenever I passed out the daily tasks, I would take the hardest one for myself, or at least not let them do it alone. I quickly found the weak links in my team and coached them to be more efficient, trying to make them better at the job.

I had one lady who was always clocking in fifteen minutes late. It got to be so consistent that management asked me to resolve the problem. I asked her nicely that she followed the schedule and was met with a carefree caviller attitude towards her start time.

No problem, I like a good passive aggressive problem. I knew that she wasn't going to change her behavior, but I needed a solution.

The following week when I made out the schedule, I changed her start time from eight o'clock to quarter past. Pushing her new departure time by the same fifteen minutes. I was happy with the solution and figured it solved both of our problems without any further conflict. I was wrong. She freaked out over the adjustment, saying that I stole the time from her. Mad at the potential of possibility having of wait to sign in until eight-fifteen. I told her that if she was ever early, I would pay her for the extra time. I had seen the sign in logs and there wasn't a single daily arrival before the new scheduled start time, so I was confident in the adjustment. She accepted the possibility of getting a few bucks for being early, and never complained to me again. She never once claimed any overtime and always showed up just after her scheduled start time, still late.

The store always got new managers. Corporate would move them around from store to store on a whim. One such afternoon the boardroom was filled with all the department supervisors, there must have been twenty of us. The chatter was loud as we all speculated on who was moved out of our store and who was moving in. The talk around the table was that he was from BC.

I chimed in "Alberta must have an asshole shortage if we are importing store managers."

The room laughed, as the new manager walked into the room. The introductions went quickly, and we were all back to work shortly after that. The whole façade was one of little substance, like they always were. My store career peaked at the supervisor level, I always joked that I wasn't a big enough asshole to get any more promotions. I wasn't interested in the power trip anyway, and even the store boss has a corporate boss. The higher you climbed the corporate ladder the less respect I had for your leadership.

After the pointless meeting I went back outside to the garden center. It was covered by a large canopy that attached to the brick wall of the store. The canopy kept the area nice and shady, and I liked the damp smell of the pavement. The pungent flowers, mixed with the smell of the hose water made me feel right at home. I would spend the afternoons reorganizing the flower trays, spreading the unsold flowers from the tall carts onto the makeshift tables and racks. The empty tall carts were in high demand and needed to be sent back to the warehouse daily to get restocked with fresh flowers. The garden center was the best part of the entire year. All the customers were friendly, excited to tell the kids about their fancy yard designs.

I always got to hire some extra help for the summer months, always choosing the most qualified personnel for the job. It's not my fault if they all happened to be cute girls. I would water the plants in the warm afternoons. The garden hose pulling at my intrusive thoughts. The spark of mischief pulling at my hand, but I never gave anyone a direct blast from the hose. I would playfully sprinkle water in their direction. Grumpy old ladies knew better than to test my resolve when I was holding the hose, they could sense my inner struggle. It was a very thin line keeping them from getting soaked. Being outside was a great way to spend the summer, it hardly felt like work, reminding me of when I had **space for golf** working at the golf course. The summer ended too quickly, and the seasonal girls went back to university to find an education.

With the season changing it was time to plan out the Christmas Garden center. I was still in charge of the hiring and brough in a team of boys to watch over the Christmas trees. I was expecting truck loads of pine trees to fill the garden center space, and some tough guys were needed to brave the cold chilly evening shifts outside.

The first truckload of trees arrived the last week of November, giving us at the store a whole month to sell them all in time for Christmas.

The fifty-foot trailers were filled floor to ceiling with the trees. I was always excited to get them unloaded and was first one on the truck when the door opened. I would pull the trees from the truck with care, handing them down to the boys on the ground. The kids would lean the trees up inside our fenced off holiday space, so we could secure them in the off hours. The trees were each wrapped in tight fishnet mesh, holding in most of the branches. The smaller trees were loaded off first and as I worked my way deeper into the truck the trees got bigger.

Once there was enough room to move around the truck, another boy would climb in and help me drag them towards the open door. We made a good team, clearing out the truck in record time, each of us knowing what to do. We had moved hundreds of trees and there were now only a few remaining along the back wall of the trailer. I picked one up and tossed it towards the open door. The adjustment string on my jackets hood got caught in the mesh. I watched as the elastic cable stretched out further than it was designed to go. The hood of the jacket shrinking around my neck. Time slowed down as I watched the plastic squeezable adjuster began to return towards my coat. It traveled at warp speed and slapped me right in the crack of my butt chin, splitting open the cold skin instantly. My body warmed up a few degrees as the shock of the impact got my blood moving faster. Drops of blood fell to the ground and were immediately noticed by the others.

"Are you alright," the boy in the truck asked, "we can finish up if you want to go take care of that." Pointing to the newly punctured hole in my face.

"No, I'm good, and were almost done" I said dripping even more crimson on the trailers floor. "And besides, I ain't got time to bleed."

Wiping the blood off my chin into the sleeve of my jacket, while not missing the opportunity quote one of the best movies of all time. Using a deeper voice to exaggerate the classic line from the Predator.

He laughed, not getting the reference. What do they teach kids these days, if they haven't even seen the Predator. We finished unloading the last of the trees from the truck and then adjusted the trees on the ground, leaning them against the fence. Before long the day was done, and we were one sleep closer to Christmas.

Road to Exile

It was early spring when I got unceremoniously exiled to the worst store in the city. I had just finished setting up the housewares department on my Thursday night evening shift for the upcoming promotion. The weasel of a store manager walked over at around eight o'clock and told me that on Friday morning I was to start at the southland store.

I was given a whole two hours of working notice of the location change. I only had one kid working with me that night and Jasmine was crushed. I was completely caught off guard, but evidently the other stores supervisor had quit out of the blue and needed to be replaced before the department promotion started. So, I needed to be there to set it up. The other store was one of the busiest in the city but was also one of the oldest buildings in the company. Its location near the train tracks made any renovations, to make it bigger impossible, so it always felt cramped and dark.

My head was spinning at the news, and I made the most of my last two hours. I had Tuesday off and planned to come back to the store and give some of my kids a proper goodbye.

I walked into the new location on Friday morning, anxious to see the state of place. The store manager barely acknowledged my existence when I went into the supervisor's common area. This was not a fun place, everyone looked like they had the life beaten out of them. The bullpen was quiet, and nobody made any noise. You could have heard a mouse fart, and I'm sure the mice were there, watching me hang my jacket on the back of my newly claimed chair.

I didn't stay long upstairs and wandered down into the back room. The store layout was reminiscent of my first store before the renovations. This gave me a strange sense of nostalgia for a place I had never been to before. I went into the back room and introduced myself to some of my inherited kids and I was instantly disliked.

The consensus was that I took the promotion away from the assistant supervisor, who felt she was ready to be the leader after the previous supervisor walked out. She wasn't, if it should have been it would have been, and I was there as the proof it wasn't her job to have. Her negative attitude filled every corner of the back room. Every person I met was cold and distant. I was left with an impossible task, but I love a good challenge, and I wasn't going to be bested at my own game.

I was undermined at every possible turn, if I said this, then they would do that. I quickly adapted and used their contempt for me to my own advantage. I was still in charge of making the schedules and rearranged the work pairs. I was unable to break up their united front, but I could make their days less enjoyable. I was a legendary troublemaker after all and a master at my craft. I wasn't going to let some bad attitudes from people I didn't really like ruin my days.

I played with the schedule for a couple of weeks and started to get some positive results. I finished the third weeks schedule and posted it before lunch, it was a work of diabolical genius. I had the whole squad timed out, so that their paths never crossed. I was happy with the achievement and wandered off to get a meatball sandwich.

When I returned from lunch the perfect schedule, that I had painstakingly crafted was vandalized with red pen and a bunch of arrows redirecting the hours. I was mad, another supervisor had over stepped and adjusted my schedule. But that's ok, I adapt quickly to adversity. Not showing my growing disdain, I worked on my strategy in the shadows.

The next week schedules were due, I didn't bother to put one up. It just so happened that our district manager was in the office later that day and asked about it.

"We need that schedule up by the end of the day." Brad said, more telling me than asking me.

"I know," I said with contempt "but I'm not doing it."

He looked up from his report with concern "Well yes, they need to be up before you go home."

"I know, but I'm still not doing it," I said holding my ground "they will just change it anyway, so they can just make the original, I'm not wasting my time." I explained, nodding in the direction of the offending supervisor.

Then I walked away, once I got down the stairs, I let out a hearty laugh, the look on Brads stupid face when I left was priceless.

When I went back upstairs at the end of the day the schedule for my department was hanging on the wall. I took a quick glance at the weeks pairings and shook my head, not impressed with the matchups.

I was going to have to adjust my strategy to get regain control of the kids. It was almost time to open the garden center, and I planned to spend the whole summer outside, so I could keep a direct eye on those who tried to mutiny my department.

I couldn't hire my own staff for the garden center this year and my outdoor haven was not subtilty filled with moles and spies. I tried to make the best of the situation but the campaign to get me to leave was taking its toll. The thought of moving on was starting to inspire the joy back into my spirit.

On one of the hotter summer days that I was fighting the urge to hose down everyone, I remembered a conversation that I had with my Uncle Grant. My Dad's brother had an extensive resume of middle management type of jobs. Our last conversation he had been raving about his latest employment as being the best job he ever held. Well, if he had the experience of lots of terrible jobs, then why would I just not start there.

I pulled out my newly acquired flip phone with the pay as you go minutes and called him from behind the forklift for some privacy. The conversation was quick and fruitful.

They were always hiring at his place of employment, and he would put in a good word. I told him that I would be by on Tuesday, my scheduled day off, and was eager to start right away. I had car payments and needed a steady flow of work to keep my bills in check. Grant practically guaranteed the job, so I closed the phone with a satisfying snap and went up to the managers office to put in my two weeks notice.

Those two weeks were magical. I was bullet proof; you can't get fired from a job if you have already quit. And if you get walked out, they had to pay you for the remaining days. I had no fucks left to give. I quit wearing the necktie immediately, I hated it anyway. I quit shaving; my beard poured out of my face. I was reminded daily by management of the requirement to be clean shaven, but never did anything about it, letting my facial hair blossom to perfection. I had received no respect from those who I was about to leave behind, and I was happy to mirror it back to them, no longer needing to hide my feelings of dislike.

On Friday I was asked by the other supervisor who always changed my schedules when I was planning to go see the third x-men movie that was starting that day.

"I got tickets for two-thirty," I said with the biggest grin.

Thomas Neamtu

I watched the wheels turn in her head, that showtime was hours before my shift was scheduled to end and she tried to work out the logistics. I walked away before she figured it out.

I went out to the garden center for one last time and watched as the daily trailer load of new flowers and plants arrived. As the air brakes on the truck let out their blast of dust moving pressure, the heavens opened and rain quickly puddled in deep holes of the beat-up parking lot.

I went back inside to get my jacket. I popped my head into the store managers office and dropped my id badge and keys on his desk.

"I don't need these until the end of the day." He said confused.

"It's the end of my day," I said with a smile, watching his frustration grow as he figured out that I was leaving early.

"You still have three more hours," he said trying to guilt me into staying. "If you leave now, I will deduct your pay, and you don't want that."

"Go for it, I wouldn't stay here for a million bucks," I said walking out the door. "And besides, I know your too lazy to fill out the paperwork."

He followed me out the door trying to punish me with a final verbal jab, but his creativity lacked inspiration, missing the chance.

"Have fun unloading that truck," I said as I passed the last window, knowing his eyes were trying to burn a hole in my back.

I got outside just as Adrianna was walking up to the store, her timing was perfect. I told her I was ready to go, and we headed off to the movie theatre to catch a matinee showing of the last stand.

I haven't been back inside that store in almost twenty years, I have no intentions of ever going back. I'm scared to see the same store manager growing dusty and old inside that corner of retail hell.

Unexpected Taxi Driver

My sister and I were going to chinook mall to have a wander through the stores. We were not on the hunt for anything, just going to browse. Chinook was the biggest mall in the city and had all the stores, you could say that it had them all. (The Mall, your welcome, I just rewired your brain.)

It had been an early spring, and the roads were still covered in a thick coating of the gravel used to provide extra traction when the snow was still on the road. I drove down Glenmore trail when the traffic slowed down for no foreseeable reason. I eased on the brakes and matched the pace of the traffic. The red taillights of the truck in front of me illuminated brightly. Traffic went from moving slowly to completely stopped without warning. The bright red taillights from the truck in front of me not giving any warning of the imminent stop as they stayed illuminated for the duration of the adjusting speeds. I pressed hard on the brakes, the car skidding on the gravel, into the back of the large pickup truck in front of us. If I had two more feet I would have stopped without any impact, but our vehicles had touched for sure. The traffic wasn't moving so I got out of my car to inspect the damage and exchange information with the other driver.

I stepped out onto the street and walked towards the back of the truck. I noticed it had city of Calgary logos down the side of the vehicle, the driver stepped out. We had a cordial interaction as we exchanged our insurance information. I apologized for the inconvenience impact and returned to my car quickly as the traffic began to creep forward again. I sat back in the drivers' seat and clicked my seatbelt into place, handing my sister the drivers information.

"Are we still going to the mall?" my sister asked.

"Yes, I want to check out the damage once we get there, it didn't look too bad, but I probably cracked a headlight." I explained.

"Perfect," she said looking up to the rear-view mirror with a suspicious glint in her eye.

I looked up into the rear-view mirror to see what she was illuding to. Much to my surprise there was a passenger in the back seat. I looked over to my sister for an explanation and she just shrugged.

Traffic was starting to move again so I couldn't turn around to have a good look at the lady in the back seat. Her fancy head scarf captured the sunlight and scattered the light like a disco ball throughout the vehicle.

"We are going to chinook; we can drop you off around there?" I asked with a confused inflection in my voice.

"Yes, I live around chinook." She said without any concern.

As we got closer to the mall, she pointed out some directions and we ended up on the street behind the mall. She indicated an apartment building to stop in front of, and I pulled the car in next to the sidewalk.

"Thank you" she said quietly as she closed the car door, rushing into the building.

I looked back over to my sister, and she just shrugged again.

"Did that just happen?" I asked, confused. "Where did she come from?" I asked.

We were parked on Glenmore trail, in the center lane, for only a few minutes. There were no pedestrian sidewalks or access to that road anywhere. It was a weird place to pickup a random person.

"I don't know," my sister started to explain "all of a sudden she was there, I didn't even see the car door open."

The door locks must have all disengaged when I stepped out onto the road, but that didn't explain where she had come from.

"Was she breastfeeding a kid back there?" I asked again, not expecting an answer.

"I think so," my sister said with a chuckle noticing my sudden uncomfortable posture.

"Let's get to the mall before we pickup any more passengers," I said as I pulled out from the sidewalk parking space.

I drove around the block and pulled into the mall parkade by the movie theatre. It was where I always tried to park. If you always use the same section of the lot, it was easy to remember where the car was when it was time to leave. I chose a brightly lit location and parked my car under the hanging lights. I got out of the car and approached the front hood expecting the worse. Much to my surprise the headlights were still intact, the only damage was a small wrinkle to the tip of the hood. When I failed to stop, I had slid the car under the raised truck. With only a crinkled hood that was barely noticeable the accident wasn't that big of a deal. After the quick inspection of the almost non-existent damage, we ventured into the mall for some lunch and shopping.

As the automatic doors parted into the malls entrance, I asked again "That lady was real, wasn't she?" "You saw her too, right?" I questioned with renewed concern of my reality.

My sister made confirmation as we walked down the hall. I was still wondering where she came from, an answer I still don't have even today. We had lunch and wandered through the stores at the mall for a few hours. We then went back home to tell our parents the tale of the mysterious breast-feeding woman who teleported into the back seat.

Unexpected Lawyer Visit

It was a Tuesday, and I had the day off work. I was down in the basement playing video games when the doorbell chimes interrupted my five-star virtual crime spree. I walked up the steps to the front landing and opened the door. I man was standing on the front steps, he was well dressed and greeted me with a smile.

"Hello, is Thomas home?" he asked with warmth in his voice.

"Yes, I'm Thomas," I said opening the screen door to greet the stranger.

"Oh great, this is for you," he said extending his arm, exposing a large envelope."

I reached out and took hold of the package "Thank you?" I said slightly confused; I wasn't expecting any mail delivery.

"You've been served." The man said loudly with glee, he then turned and rushed away before I could ask any questions.

I didn't know what had just happened and stood in the doorway for a few moments, soaking in the warm sunshine, as I processed the strange interaction. Then I went up into the kitchen to find the letter opener to tear into this oversized brown envelope. The envelope tore open with a satisfying rip, I pulled the stack of pages from the thinly sliced opening.

"Well, shit." I said out loud to myself.

I had just been sued for the accident I had with the city truck. The document said that an insurance adjuster would need to be contacted to inspect my vehicle and determine the extent of the damage caused by the impact. I didn't know how to proceed so I left the letter on the counter until my dad got home from work.

Dad and I went over the legal documents that evening, unfamiliar with the process. I made the arrangement with the adjuster to come by and have a look at the car the next day. The adjuster was over within a couple more days.

I stood on the sidewalk as he inspected the damage to my car. He had very few questions but mostly wanted to know if I had made any repairs to the vehicle. I told him no, as the only damage was barely noticeable. He used a tape measure to compare the hood alignment on both sides, making sure that the bonnet was still square. The inspection took a maximum of five minutes. We shook hands and I was told that I would be contacted about the next stage of the process within a few weeks. I watched as he drove away, anxious for the next correspondence. I had never been sued before and the unknown process was stressful, as I expected the worst.

Weeks past by until I got another letter in the mail. This one was from a lawyer's office downtown. The letter had a required appointment scheduled for the following week at the downtown lawyer's office. Dad said he would take me to the meeting, not wanting to miss an opportunity to watch me squirm and keep me out of trouble if the needed.

The day of the appointment we dressed in our most professional clothes. Dad wore his normal sports coat and a tie; I had a freshly pressed button up shirt. Funny enough these were the normal clothes we would wear to work anyway, nothing special, but perception is everything.

Dad parked in the underground parkade at Eau Clair mall, the lawyer had office space inside the market. There were a bunch of professional services taking up residence at the dying, once trendy building. We made our way up to the second floor and found the lawyers office. The receptionist was friendly and directed us into a small board room. We only waited a few moments before the lawyer showed up. He was dressed in a fancy, shiny grey suit and greeted us with firm handshakes.

"Hello, I'm going to ask you some questions that if you end up in court the prosecution will ask you." He said directly.

I nodded with understanding.

"Keep your answers short, if you say too much they are going to try and twist your words and catch you in a lie." He said.

I nodded again.

"Good, now I'm going to give you a few minutes to sit here and try to remember what happened," he said strictly.

The Lawyer pointing over to a binder that was on the long table. "That's the plaintiff's medical history; I expect you to not look inside." He said with a cheeky grin. "I'll be back in ten minutes." He turned and left the room.

The door latch hadn't even clicked, and we had the binder opened and were flipping through the pages. We learned a lot in eight minutes about the person that was suing me. The documents showed that he had previously sued everyone he could over the accident, the city, the union, workers compensation, everyone. The results from all that litigation were that the defendants all told him to pound sand. We were the last stop on his lawyered-up money train. The other driver was looking to obtain fifty thousand dollars for the damages I had caused from our accident. Good luck with that, I was living at home and had a shit retail job. It would take years for me to make that kind of money, even as a supervisor at the store. We put the binder back into position moments before the lawyer returned.

"Hello again, did you learn anything of interest while I was out?" he said with a knowing smile.

He would have been more surprised if we didn't look at the records.

"Good, so now that you know where we stand, I have some of those questions that might be asked if this ever gets into court, alright." He said rhetorically as he took his seat on the other side of the large table.

"I have a question," I said, "is he going to get the fifty thousand, I don't have that kind of money."

The lawyer smiled with reassurance "no, he probably wont, based on the past litigations. He is not suing you directly, but your insurance company. You are here on there behalf to straighten out the facts, lets start with the questions." The lawyer started, "can you tell me what happened, in your own words."

I cleared my throat and told him of the slowed traffic and then the abrupt stop. I made mention of needing only a few more feet to stop on the rocky street and this would have avoided the whole situation. I don't say anything about the mysterious woman in the back seat, I didn't want him to think I was crazy, I still couldn't explain her unexpected arrival.

He nodded and started with the next set of questions. "Were you on drugs or impaired in anyway at the time of the crash?"

"No," I said with annoyance to the question of my sobriety, but now I was definitely happy I didn't mention the mysterious woman.

He continued, noticing my discomfort, "was the sun in your eyes?"

"No," I answered

"Were you on a phone?" he pushed.

"No, I was not." I said starting to be annoyed by the simplistic questions. "I tried to stop; I slid on the gravel and a crashed into the city truck." I said relaying the story in the simplest of terms.

"So, you admit to hitting the truck?" he asked again.

"Yes, because I hit the truck." I said mater of fact.

He sat back in his chair stunned by my candor, "well, most people try to make excuses for why accidents happen, the prosecution is going to have a hard time twisting your words."

"Well, I did it, so why would I tell you any different." I said with conviction.

"I think that's all I will need from you for today, if this gets escalated into a court room, you might be called upon to testify." He explained as he gathered the binder from the long table.

"I'm still concerned about the potential payout, I barely bumped that truck, and he is claiming all sorts of physical disabilities." I asked with persistence.

"Don't worry about that," the lawyer explained, "the government has put in payout limits to low speed, low impact accident claims." "There is no way to tell how much pain some one is actually in, so for these types of incidents there is a monetary cap of five thousand dollars." "In most cases the insurance pays out some level of that money to prevent the court costs from consuming all of the plaintiff's claim." "don't worry he won't be getting rich off of this, and as I'm sure you saw, nobody is falling for his false claims of a massive injury."

I nodded in understanding "good, there is no way I caused that much damage to his body." "That big truck would have taken more impact driving over a curb than my car could have caused." "I probably could have hit him with the car directly and caused less of an injury than he was claiming."

The lawyer smiled "don't you worry about it, I'm sure this is the last you will hear about it." "The insurance company knows the score." "Thanks for coming today," he said as he ushered us out of the room.

Dad and I went back to the car, I was given a friendly reminder of safe driving practices. And a firm warning about ending up back in a lawyer's office anytime soon. Dad drove us home; I was excited to tell mom about the whole experience. Based on the information I was given I didn't expect anything more to come out of this incident. I have never heard another word on the matter since we walked out of that boardroom.

I now drive with an excessive amount of space between my car and the next one in front of me, I won't make that mistake again.

Seeing Double

Dad was outside working in the front yard. He was cleaning up the freshly cut branches of the bushes that ran the length of the property. Once a year he would trim all the bushes in the yard, sculpting their sides and flattening the branches that poked through the top.

Dad was standing on the sidewalk making sure that his handwork was aligned with his standards. Holding up his thumb to make sure the work was level and square. A neighbor from down the block was walking past the house and decided to stop for a quick visit. They chatted for a few minutes about the weather and other empty conversation fillers before the neighbor hit Dad with the verbal accusation.

"Every morning, I walk past your house, and I wave to you," she started to tell him, "I think its quite rude, you must clearly see me everyday." Her voice starting to elevate.

Dad looking confused let her continue.

"The least you could do is wave back." She finished.

Dad took a moment to diagnose the situation. He had never seen this lady before and had no idea of what she was talking about. After a few seconds Dad found his conclusion.

"That's not me," he said as mater of fact.

"Yes, it is," she companied, "I see you every day, up in the front window as I walk past the house."

"That's not me," he said again a little more forceful. "That's my evil twin, and if he sees me talking to you, he will put me back in the cellar."

She looked at him with confusion and a scowl.

Dad said with a cheeky smile. "Or maybe I'm the evil twin, I can't remember." His grin growing.

Just then her eyes drifted up to the front window of our house. Her face drained of all color as she saw my father standing up in the window looking down on them. She raised her hand just above her waist and gave a small, sheepish wave. Dad in the window didn't move a muscle, he just stood there watching over the yard.

She took a moment to compose herself, clearly shaken, then rushed away without another word to my father.

Dad hollered after her as she scurried down the street, "don't forget to wave!"

Then he turned towards the front window and waved to himself. The dad in the window still not moving, just standing there supervising from above.

Once Dad was finished in the yard, after collecting all the cut branches and stray leaves, he went into the house to get a cold refreshment. He found mom in the kitchen stirring a fresh jug of iced tea, the sides of the container covered in cold condensation.

"Well, it might be time to take me out of the front window," he explained, "my cardboard cutout is starting to upset the neighbors." He said with a big laugh, as he told my mom of the encounter on the sidewalk.

They both laughed at the absurdity of Dad having a custom cardboard cutout of himself and how it had tricked the lady down the street into thinking there were two of him.

Dad had gotten the life-size cutout of himself for his fiftieth birthday. The cardboard had been moved from room to room but ultimately took up residence in the front window. It was a great gift, bringing hours of laughter into our house. Dad would tease that for a fee you could have a picture taken with the pair of them. Some people took him up on the offer, but after the cameras flash, never paid for the silly memento.

Master of Disaster

I went to the new office to have my job interview after quitting the grocery store. The building was gigantic and looked like all the others in the industrial neighborhood. I knew nothing about the work I was about to take on. I went in blind on the tasks required and even the possible compensation. But I was free of the grocery store and that's all that really mattered.

I was hired before I even sat down. Grant had hyped me up, he was beloved inside those walls and his excitement for my addition to the team was infectious. I was thrilled and accepted the job with a firm handshake, starting immediately. I was given a wage that was substantially higher than what I received at store and even had the possibility of working overtime. At the store you were expected to work twelve-hour days but quit getting paid after eight hours. Here I was going to get paid for every hour worked and was excited to get started. I was going to be a flood and fire technician.

I got teamed up with Grant for my first few weeks. It took a great deal of energy not to call him uncle, but after awhile I broke out of the habit. It was great to work with family, I only really knew him as a kid, so getting to have adult conversations brought us closer together. As much as he and my father would dispute this fact, they were quite similar in a lot of ways. They did both fall out of the same apple tree, after all.

My uncle's friendly demeanor made it easy to work on people's home disasters. His warm smile would let them quickly know that we were there to help. It felt good being part of the solution to someone's problem. We would respond to all types of disasters, from small kitchen to fires to fully catastrophic house fires. From a leaking dishwasher to a water main break, we would help clean them all. Every day was an adventure, and no two days were even close to being the same.

One of our less dirty days we were doing a final clean on a big house in the north end of the city. It must have been summer because the kids were home from school and the parents were at work. The home belonged to a new Canadian family from Africa. The boy, probably ten years old, followed Grant around the house as he vacuumed, waiting for a chance to take over and help. I walked past the living room just as Grant handed over the vacuum hose so the excitable little guy so he could finish off the final strokes of the carpeted room.

It was almost lunch and the rest of us were in the kitchen getting some cold water. Grant joined us in the kitchen, I watched as the little guy disappeared into the basement. His older sister was on the sofa reading a magazine as the boy returned up the stairs. The sister let out a bellow of shock and covered her mouth to muffle the laughter.

We all looked over and saw the boy standing at the top of the stairs with a huge grin on his face.

"Now I can be just like the cleaners!" he said with a child's innocence.

He had powdered his face white, and his sister didn't know what to do. She scrambled to clean off his face before we saw the makeup. It was too late anyway, as we all looked up when she gasped and were trying to hold in a collective bout of hysterical laughter. Her magazine went flying as she tried to wipe the pasty makeup from his grinning face.

We cracked and started to laugh, this broke the tension, and the sister slowed the pace that she was rubbing the kids now tender cheeks. We gave her our assurance that we were not offended and thought the gesture was cute and hilarious. She took our reassurance and rushed her brother out of the room to be cleaned up properly.

It was the funniest thing I saw that year and added to another story no one would believe unless they were there. We finished cleaning the house as the sister continued to reprimanded the boy, forcing him to stay with her in the living room for the rest of our time in their house.

As the weeks went by, I got to work with the other teams. Taking the best practice from each one and adding it to my metaphorical toolbox. I took the opportunity to learn from everyone, within a short few weeks of disasters I learned a year's worth of tips and tricks to make the cleanup process quicker and more efficient.

When I returned to work with my uncle, we had a job where we needed to remove some soggy drywall from a flooded basement. We each took a room, racing to see who, would have it deconstructed first. I was in a normal sized bedroom with my box cutter knife carefully prying at the drywall, looking for the seam of the tape that divided the horizontal wall sections. The tape would normally sit about four feet from the ground, once I found the edge I pulled the tape to reveal the seam of the wall. I then cut down the wall and pulled the wet plaster off in large, controlled sections. The screws that normally held the wall in place, easily pulling through the wet plaster. I was done pulling down the soggy drywall in less than an hour.

The mess I had made was small. I quickly swept up the remaining debris, stuffing it into several of the industrial grade tear resistant garbage bags. Then I popped my head into my uncles' room. He had been busting apart the walls into small chunks. He took the demolition of every room very seriously and liked to break every piece of the wall into as many pieces as possible. I started to help, picking up the loose pieces of the scattered drywall, bragging to him of my already finished room. With a skeptical smile and a doubtful glance my uncle went to check on my work, returning quickly with bewilderment.

"How did you do that so fast?" he asked still confused by our different levels of progress.

"When Dave and I work together," I started "we work quick and clean." "Then there is less mess at the end of the day." I said, with a knowing smile.

The student was now becoming the teacher.

I tried to share all the techniques that I learned along the way with everyone. As we all know a rising tide raises all boats. This way we could all be better at the job.

I progressed along pretty good at the company. management started to indicate interest in the future potential for advancement and enrolled me in some courses. I became a certified carpet cleaning professional; I have the certificate and badge to prove it. I took a mold remediation course and became specialist in that as well. I learned a lot from the courses and was eager to put the new teachings and techniques into practice.

Whenever a containment wall or plastic door was needed, I was called in. I had mastered the erection of the plastic walls, they never sagged when I was finished. When I was a kid, I always liked to play with tape, and this was the perfect excuse to use a full roll, to keep the plastic walls secured.

My First Roommate

Dave and I were designated as the mold remediation team after we got our badges. Dave was the team lead, and I was his little helper. Dave was a foot taller than me, so I never took any offence to the little helper designation.

We got assigned to an apartment complex in Canmore, and after two weeks of commuting back to the city every day, we were put up in an apartment. The suite was part of the hotel and was the perfect space for the both of us. There was a kitchen and living room in the middle, then we each had our own bedrooms and bathrooms on the sides. We would get groceries on Monday and make our lunches in the kitchen. We would go out for dinners after our shifts as we were too tired for anything else. We got to live out in the mountains for almost two months, only returning home on weekends. I always joke that Dave was my first and only roommate.

The apartment complex was huge. It backed onto the river and after the snow melted quickly and over ran the riverbank the collective underground needed some attention. We worked out of one of the first-floor apartments. It had been completely gutted and was perfect for us to leave our tools in. the property manager had given us a key to the storage room, that was where the trap door to the underground was. The spring had come early but the sub-zero temperatures lingered. We dressed in our white hazmat suits and entered the space below the building. It was a different world down there. The darkness stretching deeper than the light provided could reach. Way off in the distance I could see a column of light penetrating into the void. We had cut a square hole in the floor of our staging apartment, so we didn't need to drag our equipment through the crawlspace. It took minutes to crawl over to the illuminated hole. The space under the building was too short to standup in, I could do a hunched over shudder step, but Dave needed to crawl. We were there to sort out a mold problem and needed to cover the ground and clean off any of the visible pipes from any possible mold contamination. The readings were high in the gutted apartment, and we needed to get the numbers back into an acceptable range.

We spent the first couple of weeks using vacuums to pull off the decade's worth of dust from the tops of the insulated pipes. Then we washed down every inch of the piping with a disinfectant solution that was too potent for commercial use. We found that the problem was all the dryer vents, from the forty first floor apartments, were all being pumped into the underground crawlspace. This caused the perfect humidity conditions for the mold to thrive. Our goal was to contain the contamination to the darkness, by closing off all the entry points to the apartments above, keeping them safe.

Dave needed a tool from back in the apartment and sent me to go get it. I moved quicker in the darkness and rushed out to absorb some sunlight. It was cold outside and the sweat inside my plastic suit froze up quickly. I thick steam bellowed off my shoulder as I walked around the building to our storage room. Dave was crawling his way to the hole we had cut into the floor so I could had it down to him. I sat at the hole and could hear him shuffling down the damp gravel towards the hole. I watched as he crawled into view. He was not looking up to see his exact position, and I reached into the hole and grabbed his head with one hand. I swear I could feel his body straighten out and leave the ground, and for a split second I held him in the air by only his head. The profanity that exited that hole was fantastically hilarious, and with the combination of threats I was laughing hard. Dave managed to spin around in the tight corridor and scurried to the trap door, determined to do me harm on his return.

The crawlspace was dark, like staring into the abyss kind of darkness. I never let my eyes wander too far past the boundary of the light, scared to see what was out there. Scared to see a pair of eyes blink back at me. The less I knew the better. Taking heed in a Friedrich Nietzsche quote "if you gaze long enough into an abyss, the abyss will gaze back into you." And I certainly wasn't interested in that.

It took Dave a solid five minutes to return to the apartment. By then he had settled down at the startle I had given him. I did feel his soul leave his body after all.

"You're lucky I had to crawl all the way back, or I would have killed you." He said half-heartedly as a warning for future jump scares. "I didn't know what grabbed me," he explained "I thought I died."

I tried not to chuckle. We had an early lunch before going back into the hole.

After the week was done, we were finished in the underground, the next step was closing off all the entry points. This was a way better task as we could stand up, for the most part. We went into each ground level apartment and sprayed a hydrogen peroxide concoction onto the pipe that disappeared into the space below. Once the fizzing stopped, we would use an expanding spray foam to permanently fill in the hole around the pipe. We went from apartment to apartment, knocking on the doors, telling them who we were and what we planned to do. All while wearing our hazmat suits and respirators hanging loose around our necks. No one seemed to be overly concerned and let us in without any fuss. I could instantly tell if the resident was a smoker when I secured the respirator into place before we sprayed the fizzy potion. The HEPA filter would mutate the smell into something even more revolting. Once we had all the apartments sealed up, we were able to vacate Canmore and return home.

Back in the Hole

I always found myself being volunteered to go into the small places the others couldn't fit. I wouldn't have that problem now; I have eaten too many cheeseburgers and have gotten kind of chunky. But back then I was small enough to fit between the floor joists and get into some tough to reach places.

Dave and I got called into the bosses' office for a special assignment. We needed to go to his house and replace the sump pump in the crawlspace. He lived next to a lake and sometimes the water would seep up into the bottom of his residence. So off we went on another subterranean adventure.

This would at least be better than the last hole I was lowered into. That one was different but not in a good way. We were called to a hotel in a small hamlet just past Canmore. A guest of the hotel had died in the bathtub with the water running, and the overflow had seeped into the depths below the room. The body was long gone by the time we arrived, but the smell wasn't. We quickly tore up the flooring and broke through the subfloor to the darkness below.

I was lowered into the hole; it was only a few feet deep. I took with me a bucket of lye, that I was going to scatter on the saturated ground. This would dissolve any lingering organic matter that might have made it into the dirt. The hole in the floor provided enough light to only see the damp ground. I didn't dare look up, I could feel the piercing eyes of past ghosts, pulling for my attention. I scattered out the lye with my rubber glove protected hands with haste. I raised the bucket out of the hole and was handed down a plastic sheet to cover the wet ground. This would give the chemical reaction a closed barrier to fester under. I placed a couple of loose rocks on the rolled-out plastic and stood up into the hole in the floor. Dave joked about closing me in the darkness, then pulled me out without any hesitations.

The boss's house was surely going to be better than that nightmare. The access was in the laundry room, the trap door barely noticeable in the busy linoleum floor pattern. The door opened with a creek as I pulled on the bronze ring latch. With the door leaved open I could see the four steps down into the crawlspace. Dave flicked on a light switch and the underground space lit up. Every corner was illuminated. This was great, no ghosts down here for sure. The ground was uneven, with the back of the house almost resting on the earth. The spaced wedged out and got deeper as the home stretched out towards the lake. We got in the hole and took stock of our situation. There was a hole in the ground with a pump in it. The hole was mostly dry, so the pump had done its job. At the deepest point of the crawl space was a wall, I peaked my head in between the floor joists and found our problem. The space beyond the wall was filled with water. There was essentially a pond under the house. Dave smiled at me, knowing there was no way he would fit through the small gap between the retaining wall and the floor. I accepted my fate and wiggled my way through the framing. Dave handed me the pump and a shovel. I dug a small hole just inside the pond to make sure the pump would be fully submerged. Remembering all the times I had pumped out the sand traps at the golf course, back when I had **space for golf**. I fished the power cable and the hose that was going to move the water back through the wall to Dave. The plan was that I would drain the pond on this side of the wall, moving the water to the sump pump and that would dispel it back outside. I turned on the pump and the hose expanded as the water was transferred to the other desired location. I watched as the pond slowly began to recede, adjusting the pump location as required. Digging deep into the water to make sure the pump never ran dry.

It was lucky that we moved all the water when we did, a few more days and the pond might have reached into the living room. It was strange being on the wrong side of a normal wall. I could see an electrical box and shuffled over to it. The light from the house slivered into the electrical box, I peered into the tiny gap and could see into the house. The plug was for a lamp in the living room, from this spot I could see the tv across the room. It was weird to see the world from this prospective, so I moved back towards the pump and moved it into its final position.

Once the pond was dry, I passed all the equipment back through the framing to Dave and wiggled and crawled through the tight spacing. It took the better part of the day to get all the water moved outside, I didn't mind an easy shift. We never knew what the next assignment was going to be, so a day of watching a pond sink, was a welcome chance to rest the body.

Perfect Aim

I had been with the company for almost two years and the days flew by. There were lots of adventures of cleaning burnt up houses, tossing toilets out of windows and all sorts of found treasures along the way.

I was teamed with Dave again for another huge apartment fire. This one was in town, so we didn't have to spend every waking minute together. The building fire was caused by a careless cigarette, a flowerpot and a leaking propane tank on a barbeque. The subsequent fire had burned up six of the third-floor apartments. The firefighters flooded the other eighty-four, making sure the fire wasn't in the walls. It was going to be other months worth of work at a single location, the consistent nature of the task was welcome. We had to help the tenants without insurance pack up their apartments, so the rooms would be completely empty for the restoration. I was surprised at how many people didn't have any insurance at all. The tenants with insurance would be relocated for the duration of the work, but those without, would have to fend for themselves. It took full week to pack out the apartments.

We then had to remove every fridge from the building. The power had been out since the night of the fire and everything inside the fridges had expired and turned into moldy abominations. Curiosity only pulled at me once and I peeked inside the dark fridge. The smell that emanated almost knocked me over. It reminded me of the time we had to clean a house fire. I found a kid's lunch box under his bed. I thought it might have some keepsakes worth cleaning, so I popped the silver hinge. I was mistaken and almost had an involuntary protein spill on my steel toe boots. That lunch must have been under the bed for years, the sandwich waved goodbye as a shut the lid with disgust. After the mistake I make in looking inside we made sure to secure the fridge doors with multiple wraps of our packing tape. We started at the furthest point and trucked out the fridges. It was best to move the long-haul units first, when we had the most energy at the start of the day. We moved fridges for three days straight, one floor each day.

Then we went and removed the doors off every apartment. The fire department had the key for every room and used the boot key on every door. The door frames were shattered and would all need to be replaced. The apartment doors were heavy and took teamwork to carry them out.

Our next step was to pullout all the carpet and baseboards. The rooms were starting to look desolate as we pulled them apart. Some of the rooms still had abandoned items and those needed to be discarded as well. Dave and I were working up on the third floor in one of the apartments that were affected by the fire. We were planning on spending the whole day moving out the burnt-up items. The roof was gone, it was strange to have the blue sky above us as we worked. I had gone into the bedroom to pickup all the clothes that were left behind with their crispy edges. I filled the garbage bag quickly as the volume of clothes was vast. While moving through the room I uncovered a large rubber chest and peaked inside. A big smile crossed my lips. Dave was in the other room and with no roof there was not really any boundary between us. I reached into the rubber chest and pulled out some of the toys. I began to toss the multicolored rubber dildos over the wall and shouted.

"It's raining dicks!" as I burst out laughing.

Dave must have looked up, just in time for one to land on his head, before he could muster a "What?"

The bucket was full to the top with the sex toys, I lobbed ten or twelve over the wall in Daves direction until I could hear him start to laugh. One of the other teams heard the commotion and wondered over to see what was going on. The room was littered with a variety of dicks, all shapes and sizes. Dave picked up the one that hit him in the head and chased the snooping coworker down the hall. I watched from the doorway and laughed until my sides hurt. Moments like that helped to bring some levity to the harsh fact that we were cleaning up someone's worst day. After we finished with the jokes, we went back to work and finished the day.

After weeks of getting all the apartments gutted down to the drywall it was discovered that there was asbestos in the walls. If it was contained behind the drywall, we were safe. Another company was called in, they only specialized in the hazardous removal and took care of all the wall removals. Dave and I got reassigned.

A Family Connection

Dave and I got sent out to Bowness to clean up a leaky roof flood. The water had poured out of the attic access door and into the kitchen. The water was easily cleaned up, but all the insulation was soaked up in the ceiling. Being the smallest, I was nominated to go up and vacuum out all the dusty grey fiberglass. I put on my white hazmat suit and taped up the cuffs of both the arms and legs. I wanted to keep out as much of the itchy material as possible. It was late august and was hot outside, and even hotter at the top of the house.

I was instantly covered in sweat, as I crawled to the back of the small space. Dave stood on the ladder with the vacuum balanced on the top. He pushed the hose towards me, and I took hold. The space cramped and having the vacuum up there wasn't going to work. I had to watch my footing and only put pressure on the ceiling joists, or I would fall through. The vacuum echoed in the enclosed space, and I hated every minute of it. I had been in a lot of uncomfortable places over the last two years but this one broke me.

I was too hot; my clothes were soaked and my whole body itched from the unstoppable fiberglass. I did the job, daydreaming of a time where I wouldn't be stuck in the attic, and hoped that it arrived soon. But I worked almost every day so going to find a new job was going to be challenging. Once the last chunk of that torturous material was sucked out of the ceiling our day was done. I discarded the paper suit and could hardly wait to get home for a cold shower. My body was starting to turn red with a rash from the insulation and the cold water would feel wonderful.

That night at family dinner as we sat around and ate Dad told us that his inside person had put in their notice.

"Hey, why don't you come work for me?" Dad asked with a smirk.

He had hated the work I was doing. Sure, it was good work, but it was dirty work. We worked with cleaning chemicals and Dad didn't like that. He always blamed the origin of his cancer from working at the batter plant and being around all the chemicals there. So, he wanted me to come work for him. This was almost serendipitous, as I had spent the afternoon dreaming of a way out.

"I have to know by Monday, or I'm putting an add in the paper." He explained giving me a deadline.

I knew better, from having past jobs, that I should ask some questions.

"What kind of work will I have to do?" I asked. I had worked for Dad, as a summer job a few years back and wanted to know if I was going back into the shop. "What does it pay?" I said with a smile. Having my mind already made up.

"It will be in the office." He explained, "you will take orders, and answer the phone." "As for the pay I will start you at five bucks an hour more, than you are getting now."

"Sounds good to me." I said enthusiastically. It was a perfect moment in time, where the stars aligned. "I will have to give them two weeks notice." I said holding true to my responsibility.

"Sure, that will work." Dad said with a big grin.

I had my own selfish reasons for taking a job with my father. His heath was more inconsistent these days and his time was running out. So, any extra moments I could have would be treasured.

I went into work on Monday with the intention of putting in my resignation. I had hyped myself up as I drove to the office, I was focused and ready. I walked though the shop; past all the tables of property we needed to wash. I was walking quickly, with purpose, when Grant stepped out in front of me.

"Happy Monday," he greeted "I had the strangest dream last night."

I stopped, "happy Monday," I greeted him back, my focus momentarily broken. "What did you dream this time?" I asked expecting some wild tale of danger and adventure.

"I had a dream that you were quitting" he said with a look of concern and a slight frown.

With confusion on my mind, I told him "Well, yes I am, that is exactly what I'm going to do right now."

I don't know how he knew that the decision was only made on Friday, and I hadn't told anyone yet. Grant and my father didn't call each other often so I doubt the news came from my dad.

Grant tapped at his head "psychic." "Something better I hope," he asked his frown quickly turning to a smile.

"Give me five minutes, and I'll tell you all about it," I said as I rushed into the office not wanting to lose my nerve and make the situation harder.

The news was met with disappointment but understanding. I was told that I would always be welcomed back and wished well on the new job. I thanked the boss for all the opportunity and for the education provided and left the office quickly. I returned to Grant to tell him about going to work with my dad.

That was almost twenty years ago and the psychic connection between us must still be active. As I wrote the master of disaster story of this book, I got a text from my uncle. I hadn't got a message from him in almost a year, and the timing was eerie. I was trying to focus into the past and tell a story of us working together, and at that exact moment he sends a message. Wild. So, I guess if I have been thinking of you, and you begin to tingle, now you know why. Psychic Powers.

The End is Nigh

I went to work for my father. The office building was a remnant of the seventies. The building was a time machine, with outdated furnishings. The pink porcelain of the sink and toilets in the washrooms were an exceptionally nice throw back. Dad had found a discarded picture of Elvis and hung it in the bathroom. Elvis would watch over your shoulder when you washed your hands, it was the perfect accent to the place.

I settled in quickly, enjoying the quality time with my dad. The consistent schedule made life predictable. Each day was still different, with unique challenges, but a Monday to Friday job gave me back my freedom from being on call.

Before long the company was purchased by a collective that acquired like minded businesses. Not long after that they purchased the competition, and we moved into their building.

Dad was running a successful business and was given the duty to run the newly acquired workforce. It was a strange moment in time. Dad had started his career at the newly acquisitioned business, and this was seen as a homecoming of sorts. His return was a full circle to where it all began, from a job he left decades before. We brought Elvis with us.

Dads' legend proceeded him, and the staff was uncertain of his temperament. He was known as a ruthless businessman, who could turn you to dust with just one sideways glance. I found it interesting to see how others viewed his arrival. They quickly learned the truth, that he had adapted well and had mellowed with age. He met them with kindness, understanding and respect. He wasn't there to piss on their legacy, we were there to build a new one on the decades of established groundwork. The business would be better than it ever was when we were apart, and the future was bright.

I adapted quickly to the new coworkers and was excited to be part of something with a rich history and the potential of having a great future.

We had a few good years in that building, adapting to the changing markets. Our parent company was building us our own location just outside of the city limits. The ground was broken, the foundations were poured and a scheduled move in date was marked on the calendar. That's when the wheels fell off.

Dads' health had taken a turn. He had been battling cancer for most of my life and the peaks and valleys of his condition were a normal part of our days. In his true stoic fashion, he never let on to how bad it was, ever. He and my mother would face the demons together, shielding my sister and I from the reality of the horrible situation. They did this for our whole lives. Keeping us in the dark on the dire nature of the diseased reality. The truth was he had been dying for the better part of twenty-five years, and we were just so accustomed to being on the edge of despair, that it was just our normal functioning frequency.

Dad could see the end in sight and didn't plan to be around for another year. My sister got pregnant and that pushed him to fight again. He wanted to obtain the title of grandfather and pulled himself back together. We went to Vegas for Christmas that year, having a fantastic break from tradition. Dad put on a brave face as were wondered through the hotels and casinos. His excitement for each day was maximised with an itinerary that kept our feet sore and our minds off the inevitable. It was a great holiday filled with no worries and much laughter.

When we got back home, I found out Dad had a lump in his groin, right where the leg attaches to the hip. You would have never known that every step he took in Vegas caused such excruciating pain, but he was made of steel after all, and you can't hurt steel. He had been through so much pain over the years that he could withstand a pain that most people will never understand.

My sister had some heartbreaking news and Dad's promotion to grandfather was delayed for a year. He fought on, unwilling to shuffle off this mortal coil, until he got his promotion. Life went on with death waiting in the corner, extending the courtesy of not taking my father for a few more months.

Dad had his fifty-fifth birthday cake in January, and we celebrated another successful revolution around the sun. A few short days later a Monkey was hatched, and Dad got his long-awaited promotion. We welcomed the blessing.

Dads' health detreated quickly after that; the next few months were spent taking him to appointments trying to manage his pain. Until he was admitted to the hospital for the final few days.

Mom would spend every possible moment at his side. I tried to go to work to take my mind off the inevitable, but I couldn't make it down the street. I tried to, but it was like two magnets fighting against each other, I physically couldn't make it down the street. Work was understanding and gave me the time off.

I went to the hospital and visited with Dad as best we could. Watching my father dying in front of my eyes was devastating. He had a few last-minute pieces of business that he wanted us to attend to, and then knowing everything was taken care of, he would be free to go.

One of his requests was that I stay living at home a bit longer, so my mother wouldn't be alone. I had started to look at moving out and quickly agreed to put those plans on hold.

Then he wanted all the funeral arrangements to be handled, while he waited for his number to be called. Mom and I agreed and left his bedside to go make the final arrangements.

The funeral home experience was luckily a unique one, and we went inside without any expectations. The director was kind enough to get us through the process, as we joked and tried to make light of the looming situation. Dad was still living after all, so we weren't in mourning, and the morbid jokes we made throughout the visit were a welcome change for the funeral director. The funeral director gave us the grand tour, telling us what to expect and was grateful for our open candor. Most of the visitors she met with were dealing with one of their worst days, and we weren't there yet. The dark humor was a welcome addition to the experience. We had the event planned and returned to my father to tell him of the progress. When the news met his ears, you could see the stress leave his body. We watched him relax, knowing that everything after his departure was going to be ok. We stayed for a while by his side as the sunset, using every possible minute of the allowed visiting hours.

I had made my peace and didn't plan to return the next day, but I was compelled for a final visit and went back unable to stay away. I sat by his side and held his shrinking hand for as long as I could muster.

Mom stayed, never leaving his side. By the time I got home mom called, asking for my return. Death had finally come to collect him. I returned to the hospital with a deep sadness in my heart. I found my mom outside the room wearing her bravest face, but just because the tears had been wiped away, their stained tracks remained. We had a hearty embrace, and I wept in her arms until my sister arrived.

She told us of how he was ready and that in time we will see this as a good thing. She told us of his last moments. How dad was awoken from his rest, looking past her into the corner.

He verbally agreed to an unasked question, then breathed his last breath, drifting off into the piece of the unknown. We stayed in the hospital for a while until we were ready to go home.

I walked down the hallway towards the elevator with my head held high and a burning lump in my throat. My eyes welled with tears, but none fell. This wasn't the place for that, there would be time later to drop some tears.

How Can Silence Be So Loud?

The next few days were a blur as we waited for the funeral of my father. We arrived early at the funeral home after being picked up by a limousine. I was in no shape to drive and happily took the ride. I stood by the front doors, wearing my dark suit taking a moment to compose myself as the mourners arrived. Hundreds of people showed up and I greeted every one of them with a firm handshake and an occasional hug. I accepted their condolences and directed them over towards my mother and sister.

The day was a blur, I don't remember many of the sad faces, but I do remember their warm words of comfort. I had cried all my tears the week before so at the funeral only a single tear fell from my eye. Mom was in the same state, strong and focused. She was going to mourn in her own way, far from the prying eyes looking for gossip.

Some old friends showed up and we reminisced on better days. We laughed at stories of my father and how he had been a positive affect on everyone that got to know him.

Bayley had a great story about my father, and we laughed hard at the retelling. He had gone to get his bike repaired downtown and the keys to Bayley's parent's mini van were accidently locked inside. Mike and I went with him on the adventure, Bayley had parked the van a few blocks from the store and pushed the bike in for the required repair. Once the bike was booked in, we walked back to the van not noticing the error of the missing keys until we got back to the parking lot.

Cell phones didn't exist yet, so Bayley wandered down the block looking for a pay phone. Mike and I stayed back at the vehicle and waited for his return. Bayley found a working pay phone on the corner two blocks over. He dropped in the quarter, the cost needed to make a call and dialed the first number that came to mind.

"Hello," my dad answered.

"Hello, its Bayley, can you come get us?" he started to explain "the keys have been locked in the van."

"Do you have an extra quarter?" Dad asked, his grin must have been huge from the setup.

"Yes, I do, why?" Bayley asked, not yet seeing the punchline.

"Good, call someone who cares." Dad said as he hung up the phone, probably with a giggle.

Bayley stood there for a moment contemplating his next move and decided to call back. My dad was challenging, but his dad was harder to reach, something so trivial as the keys wouldn't pull him out of one of his undercover missions. So, Bayley dropped his second quarter and called back.

"Hello," my dad answered quickly on the first ring.

"Hello, its Bayley, can you come get us?" he said with a tone of urgency. "Please, old man, i need to get home to use the spare key." "I need to have the van back before my parents get home from work."

"Where are you?" Dad asked, slightly annoyed.

Bayley gave him the cross of the streets where he was standing and hung up the phone. Then he walked back towards us, excited of my dad's expected arrival.

Dad traveled downtown and found the corner with the pay phone, Bayley wasn't there. He drove the around the block looking for us. Bayley still wasn't at the corner where the call was made from, when dad made his second pass. By the time he found us Dad was grumpy, it made for a humorous ride home as he lectured Bayley on how to give directions.

We had all been calling my father "old man" for years. It was our term of endearment for him and after awhile he no longer took offence. Thinking back on it now, I see it as just one more blessing, us calling him an old man, as it turned out to be something he would never get to be. Dad passed away at fifty-five. He always talked about his freedom fifty-five and that year he found it, maybe he always knew, but the coincidence still stands.

After a nice service and some tiny sandwiches, we were driven back home. Some of the family followed the limo back to the house, for more sandwiches and sympathies. We all sat around the house for a few more hours until our guests were satisfied with their attempts to bring us comfort. For the most part they were successful, giving us a few short moments to forget about the loss. After a few short goodbyes the house was empty.

It was just my mother, and I left, standing in the living room. The sweet smell of flowers filled the house. My ears rang from the emptiness of the place, how can silence be so loud. We didn't speak on the weight of the day and just went into a robotic response of readjusting the house back to its normal state.

Facing the Ghosts

I went back to work on Monday. The force that kept me away the week before had vanished and I could finally make it down the street. The office was surprised at my quick return and asked if I needed any bereavement leave. I declined the offer and explained that I used that time the week before visiting with my dad in the hospital. Explaining those moments with my father in the remaining days were quality time. I could have spent the next week being broken up about the loss, but I had cried all those tears already. I needed the distraction now, and putting some energy into my work seemed like it was my best option.

The darkened office that was my dads brought some sadness to my heart, but we hadn't been in the building that long, so his spirit didn't have a chance to take hold over the space. At around nine thirty there was a commotion at the front door.

A squadron of Hutterites burst into the office, demanding to see my father.

"I'm here to see Glen." The oldest man demanded.

I relayed the tragic news as the oldest of the bearded men held up an obituary.

"I didn't believe it." The man said with sadness in his eyes. "I have known Glen a long time," the man explained, "your father was unkillable."

I assured him of his passing, but they demanded to go into his office. Before I could object the four men were in dad's office. I followed them, the darkened room down the hall gave them no better answers. One of the men even checked under the desk, as if my father was hiding as a joke. I wished that was the case.

They returned with me back to my desk with saddened defeat. I handed them a funeral pamphlet and wished them well. They departed the building with their heads held low, but as the left I could hear a mumbled voice say, "but he was unkillable."

Every customer had a story for me. I absorbed them all, eager to hear the past tales of my father. Most people had stories of how they liked and respected my dad. Stories of their positive interactions and how he had helped them in the past. Other people had stories of how they didn't like my father. These were the tales I was the most interested in. I would listen with great focus, pressing the phone firmly into my ear, not wanting to miss a single breath of the story. If the intent of the story was to cause me discomfort, they failed, I loved every beat of the hard interactions. If the storyteller ended the conversation by saying how much they didn't like my dad, I would retort by telling them that he didn't hold them in very high regard either. It felt like justice for past transgressions and made me feel better.

I still continue to get dads stories even now, but they are becoming less frequent, as the people that knew him started to retire.

Back at the house, ghosts would call the home phone every night. My dad always traveled for work; any given year he spent more hours in the car then most people spent in the office. His regular time to call home was around seven o'clock. The phone would ring around that time every night. Dad would be on the other end of the line, ready to quickly tell me about his day before I would pass the call over to my mother for a lengthy conversation. But after the funeral every time the phone would ring after seven, my heart would jump. The expectation of dad being on the other end was powerful. I would race to answer the phone, half expecting to hear his voice on the other side. The pit of my stomach would drop when it was never him calling. This went on until I moved out. I never call my mother in the evening, always in the mornings for just this reason.

There were new challenges waiting to test my grief around every corner. I couldn't go to our favorite Chinese restaurant without it feeling like something was missing. The food never changed but it never quite tasted the same. We would still get the family discount, but it was never like it once was. When the restaurant changed locations, we went for a few meals, but the magic was gone. Now we couldn't go even if we wanted to, some crazy person burnt down the building, and it never reopened.

Years later I even got ambushed by a ghost at a hockey game. I walked through the metal detector, placing my wallet and keys into my hat as I passed through. I replaced my keys in pocket, standing tall on my tips of my toes, stretching to see if I could find the shortest pop corn line. A friendly person wearing a bright red jersey and a big smile approached, asking if wanted to purchase a program for tonight's game. The question almost dropped me to my knees. My legs buckled; I needed a moment to compose myself. I declined the offer and rushed off to lean on a pillar. It took a great deal of focus to hold the tears within my eyes. I had always gotten my father a program from the hockey game, and the simple question caught me off guard.

Over time I have decided to enjoy these types of moments. Whenever a sliver of grief pierces my heart, I try to see them as a reminder of the good old days. These moments are not something that needs to be feared. I bring up my father often in conversations, not shying away from the topic. As long as we keep telling the stories, he will be with us forever.

He visits me in my dreams sometimes, helping me to resolve lingering problems that have crept into my brain. Some of the imaginary problems don't exist and never have, but his words of wisdom are always welcome. When I awake from those sleeps, I'm happy with the memories of the past.

It's been almost fifteen years since his passing and time has healed most of the wounds. I was lucky enough to be in an environment after his passing that wasn't afraid to speak his name, welcoming the positive stories and tales of the grievances. This gave me the armor required to take on the world without fear, knowing that he would never be forgotten and besides no one shook the ground like my father did.

Two Weeks of Silence

It was the middle of summer and Dad had a business trip to Saskatchewan. He took my mother with him for the week. She planned to spend the days with her parents and visiting her sisters. Dad would work out in the territory then join her for the evening visits with family.

The garage door had just closed and the taillights from dad's car hadn't even reached the bottom of the street yet, when my sister ran down the stairs. She was way too excited, and her presence was disrupting the movie I was trying to enjoy.

"Can you take me somewhere?" she asked with a grin.

"Where?" I asked, as an uninterested brother would.

"I made an appointment to get my belly button pierced." She said, smacking her belly with excitement.

"Where?" I asked, as partially interested brother would.

"Over by the university," she squealed, knowing that I would soon agree to her planned excursion.

"Sure, lets go." I said, excited to go for a drive. My yellow Camero sat in the driveway ready to go.

We drove down the winding streets towards the university, the horsepower of the car anxious to chirp the tires at every opportunity. We got to the tattoo and piercing shop and went inside. I recognised the lady behind the counter, she was one of the waitresses at the golf course. Her husband owned the shop, he did the tattoos, she did the piercings. My sister must have made this plan the week before, while she was working in the restaurant's kitchen. The room was not very big and only had a few stations setup for the body modifications. My sister was guided to one of the padded tables and took a seat. There wasn't much conversation. I watched my sister get a needle poked through her belly flesh. As the needle was pulled through the puncture a ring followed behind. My sister let out a deep breath, but not a yelp of pain, and then they were done.

The attention quickly turned in my direction. I looked around to see if something more interesting was behind me. Nope, just me.

"What are you going to get pierced?" the waitress asked with a maniacal grin. "You can get whatever you want, and I'll punch the hole for free." "You just have to pay for the jewelry."

That's when my sister interjected, "I'll pay for the ring." Her smile from ear to ear.

I hadn't woken up today with any intentions of having an extra hole punched in my head, but hey why not. The ear lobe was out of the question. I pulled at the top of my ear.

"How about here?" I said with more uncertainty than confidence.

"Ah, the helix," the waitress said, "great choice, have a seat."

I traded places with my sister on the padded table and braced myself for a blast of pain. I could feel the cold steel pierce my ear as it was pulled through, but it didn't really hurt. Once the loop was closed, my body got warm, and I felt a powerful surge of life. I felt great, and that feeling lingered for days. My sister squared up the tab and we went back home.

The week went by fast and on Friday my parents returned. Mom wasn't even in the house yet and my sister had her shirt lifted to show off the new addition to her belly button. Mom wasn't impressed. Evidently my sister had asked if she could get her belly pierced and mom had given an emphatic no to that request. Dad had joined mom on the front step to see what was going on, just as I was walking out the front door to greet them.

My sister looking around for a scape goat blurted out, "Well Thomas got his ear pierced."

Well shit, all the attention was removed from her and turned in my direction. I tried to go back into the house but was called forward. Dads' eyes quickly targeted the shiny metal ring hanging in my ear. His arm reached out to grab the loop. I backed up and deflected the attempt.

"That's not real," Dad said with certainty. "It has to be fake!" "It's a trick, some sort of costume jewelry." He said trying to adjust his reality.

I pulled at the ring, and it tugged my ear. Dads' eyes got big, and he got mad.

He didn't know what to do, so he just shook his head and said, "stupid." "Stupid, stupid," he repeated.

Then went back to the car to bring in their luggage.

We had planned to go for dinner upon their return and departed for the restaurant. Dad sat at the table quietly, only talking with the waitress to place his order.

Mom was busy telling my sister about her disappointment in the bad choices we had made while they were away.

I tried to ask Dad how the week went, but he would only shake his head and mutter, "stupid, stupid."

This went on for weeks, Dad giving me the silent treatment.

Years later whenever I wanted to get, I rise out of him I would ask if he was still bothered by the earring.

He always answered "yes."

I always answered, "good, then I'll keep it in for another year."

This piece of steel has been in my ear for almost twenty-five years, I don't see it as a part of my personal identity, but I have no intention of getting rid of it. Truthfully the only time I think about it is when the barber catches the ring with a stary comb, giving it a forceful, somewhat unpleasant tug.

A short time later at the mall we got Dad good. My sister was getting her second hole punched in her ear lobe. Dad and I, were standing outside the shop, watching the carnage through the window. The technician loaded the piercing tool and wiggled it into position. Dad took a deep breath as she pulled the spring-loaded handle, waiting to see the pain shiver across my sister's face. Just as the handle made the loud click, I flicked the back of dad's ear with a well-timed stinging smack. Dad turned; his eyes stretched big with fear.

"What did you do?" he said, shaking more than usual, "you pieced me, I'm tagged."

Dad's mind raced as he contemplated having an earing. He wandered off to the mall bench and had a seat. My mom and sister wandered over to us. My sister showing off her new stud earrings.

"What's wrong with Dad?" Lisa asked.

Dad looked up, eyes still full of fear, holding his ear. "He pieced me, I'm tagged."

I laughed "He thinks I gave him an earing."

Dad looked over at me, "I'm not pierced?"

"No, why would I do that old man," I said.

"I'm not pierced," he said with a bit more conviction, but still confused by the pain. "But, but..." he stammered.

"it's all in the timing," I grinned, mimicking the flicking motion with my fingers.

He turned to my mom, dropping his hand, having her check for any extra holes in his ears. She made the confirmation, then he made her check again just to be sure.

It was always good fun to give dad a hard time. Those were the best days, playing tricks and poking fun.

Thomas Ncamtu

Epilogue

I have always been trying to shake the ground like my father. Making a dent in the universe and fighting the system whenever possible. Rebelling against authority and trying to impose my will to cut through red tape and endless redundancy. This made me a difficult person to deal with at times. I forced the world around me to change, not much, but enough.

I hope these stories have changed you in some way. I think my father would be proud to read these tales, remising of the good old days and making jokes about why I only have six lives left. And hey! Where are my shoes.

Thomas Neamtu

In loving Memory of Glen Neamtu

1955 – 2010

Thomas Neamtu

Special Thanks

Thank you to everyone who pushed me forward with praise and encouragement. Telling these stories has been a magical trip down memory lane. Having the chance to reminisce about my favorite times as a troublemaker has brought me great joy, hopefully giving you a laugh or two.

Thank you to everyone who inhabits my tales of mischief, I couldn't tell my stories without telling some parts of yours. If you are dissatisfied with your portrayal, too bad, go write your own book. I'd be happy to help if you wanted to collaborate.

Thank you to everyone who has taken the time to read the pages that I have assembled, your support means the world to me. I will blame all future projects on you, as your positivity fuels my creative fire, pushing me to create even more.

Thomas Neamtu

Other Titles Available

SPACE FOR GOLF

WRITE YOUR SECOND BOOK IN 236 STEPS OR LESS

Six Lives Left
Hey! Where Are My Shoes?

Thomas Neamtu